Drawing Closer to Allah and His Prophet: A Practical Guide

Dr Abdul Qader Ismail

Drawing Closer to Allah and His Prophet: A Practical Guide
(second edition - ISBN 978-1739670535)

Written by Dr Abdul Qader Ismail BMBCh (Oxon), MA (Oxon), MRCPCH, under the spiritual guidance of Khwaja Muhammad Ulfat Qadri Naqshbandi (Lahore, Pakistan), and Pir Mohammad Tayyab Ur-Rahman Qadri (Qadria Trust, UK; Bhera Shareef, Haripur, Pakistan).

Back cover photo by PhotoLanda.

My thanks to Mr Omar Chaudhry and Mrs Atheah Gsouma for their help in proofreading the text.

May Allah (Almighty) accept the charity of everyone who donated to allow us to print and distribute this book to our Muslim brothers and sisters in prison.

Please pray for the late Ch. Abdul Rehman, Muhammed Azam, Zafar Iqbal, Mohammed Usman and Tahir Ahmed. May Allah (Almighty) forgive their sins and grant them Jannah. Ameen.

This project would also have not been possible without the help and support of Himaya Haven. Special thanks go to Imam Haroon Shafiq, Imam Saqib Hussain, Imam Nasam Hussain and Project Unite of HMP Oakwood Prison.

May Allah (Almighty) allow them to continue being the means by which He bestows mercy upon His creation.

Special Duas for all those who lost their lives, homes, and loved ones during the Turkey/Syria earthquake of February 2023.

All English translations of Qur'anic passages are taken from 'The Majestic Quran' (ISBN 978-1902248776)

Designed by Toqeer Bhatti
www.synergidigital.com

For my precious parents and beloved wife.

Contents

Foreword 6

Purity of Self: Avoiding the stain of sins 11

The Qur'an: Reciting, understanding, and internalising it 59

The Salah: Praying with Khushu 89

The Sunnah: Celebrating our Prophet by following his example . . 129

Sending peace and blessings upon the Prophet 153

Fasting: Training our Nafs and increasing our Taqwa 181

Charity: Investing in this life and the next 211

The Divine Decree: Finding peace through acceptance 235

Foreword

The religion of Islam is about submission to the Lord of the Universe, seeking His pleasure and serving His creation. Submission to Allah and serving others are the activities of a practicing Muslim. Dr Ismail has very thoughtfully put together a set of Islamic practices that will help the reader achieve these goals. This is not your typical religious text which you can read and forget about, but a practical guide which provides detailed checklists, engagement with which can help change a person's life.

The author has confined himself to the major practices that really bring about a change in a person's thinking, devotional habits and experience of Islam. Therefore, he has chosen purity of self, the reading of the Qur'an, the daily prayers, following the beautiful example and sending peace and blessings upon the blessed Prophet (peace be upon him), fasting, charity, and finally, accepting the Divine Decree to achieve peace and happiness. The checklists challenge, and make the reader reflect on their own daily habits and practices to help bring about change, to help you draw closer to Allah and His Prophet (peace be upon him). I commend Dr Ismail for this innovative and effective approach.

Dr Musharraf Hussain Al-Azhari (OBE, DL) CEO & Chief Imam Karimia Institute

Introduction

In modern times, especially for those born into Muslim families, religion has become a ritualistic hobby. We follow customs, perform acts and recite prayers without understanding the significance of what we are doing. We attend religious gatherings but what we hear does not translate into strengthening our faith or changing our behaviour. Practicing this kind of 'superficial' Islam means we fail to receive its full blessings and are more likely to neglect our faith and move further away from Allah in times of difficulty or when we are busy with worldly matters. Furthermore, if we do not practice the faith with understanding, what example are we setting others, especially non-Muslims? And what will we be able to teach our children?

The purpose of this book is to provide you with the means to change your thoughts and behaviour regarding some of the most fundamental aspects of religion. Each chapter introduces a topic using the Qur'an and Hadith followed by practical advice on how to act upon this; recording daily/weekly/monthly progress in the space provided. Sincere engagement with this process will help you develop lifelong habits of practicing your faith, understanding why you are doing what you are doing.

Each chapter is independent of the others therefore the book does not need to be read in any specific order. However, I would advise you to focus on one chapter at a time, and try not to do too much too soon since you are likely to overburden yourself and disengage with the process. Remember the words of the Prophet (peace be upon him):

> *"Take up good deeds only as much as you are able, for the best deeds are those done regularly even if they are few." (Ibn Majah)*

Use this book with the firm intention to better yourself in the hope of pleasing and drawing closer to Allah and His Prophet (peace be upon him). Certainly, Allah will help you:

> *"He who draws close to Me a hand's span, I will draw close to him an arm's length. And whoever draws near Me an arm's length, I will draw near him a fathom's length. And whoever comes to Me walking, I will go to him running..." (Bukhari)*

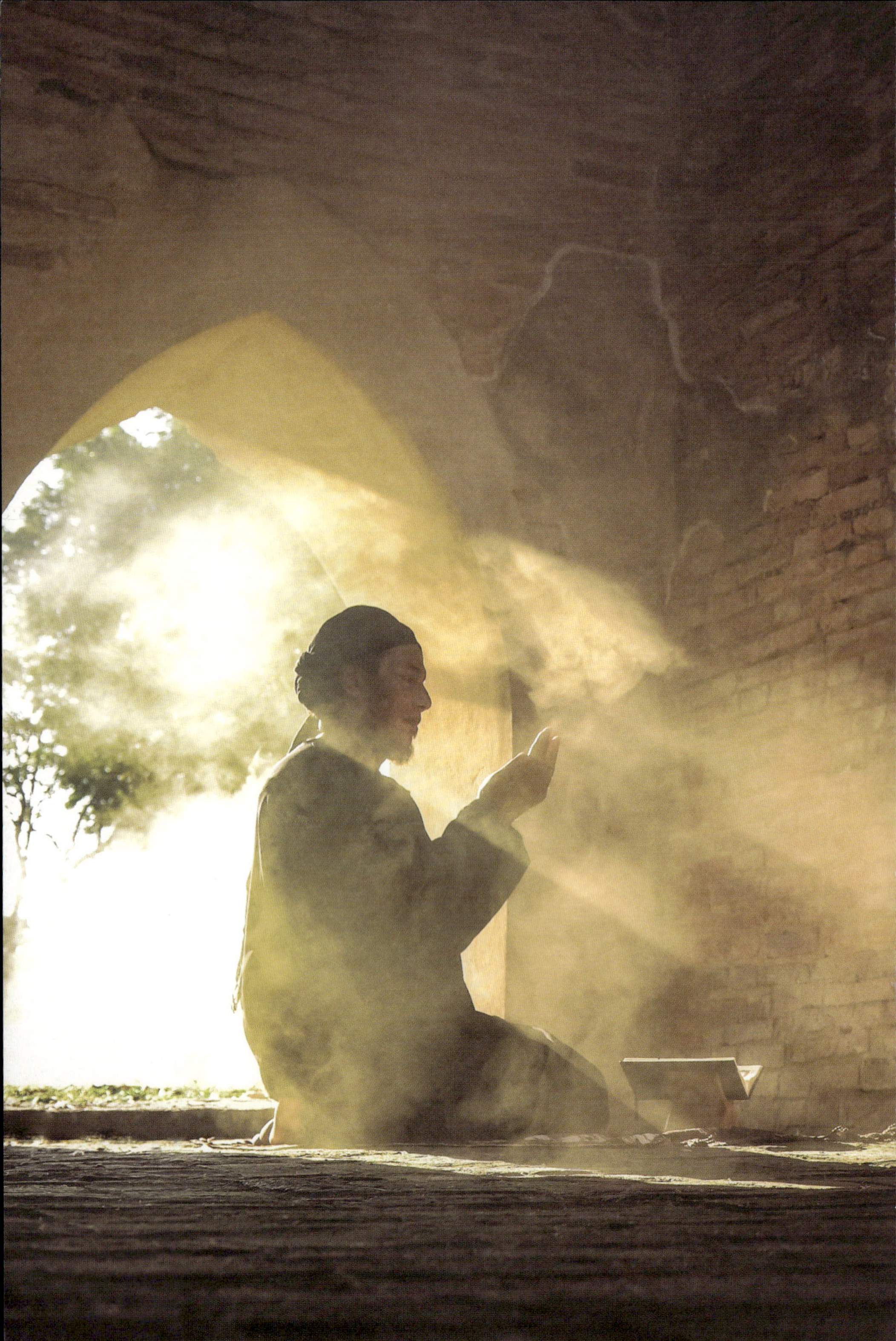

Purity of Self: Avoiding the stain of sins

What makes us commit sins?

We have two arch-nemeses: our Nafs (in its untrained form – the Nafs al-Ammara or the 'commanding soul') and Shaitan (the devil). The Nafs is the part of our self/soul, which produces 'animal' desires within us; to eat, drink, sleep, find comfort, be lazy, lust and procreate; whether by Halal (permissible) or Haram (impermissible) means.

It is through encouraging the untrained Nafs that the devil encourages us to indulge ourselves and sin; discouraging us from putting in the effort to perform good deeds. If we let this Nafs take over and follow its every desire then we are no better than animals, in fact we are worse because they have no choice but to act upon their instincts, whereas we have a degree of self-control, and therefore, choice.

> *Do you think you can be a guardian of someone who makes his desires, god? Do you reckon they listen to you, or reflect? They are like cattle. No, in fact they are even further astray from the straight path. (Qur'an 25:43-44)*

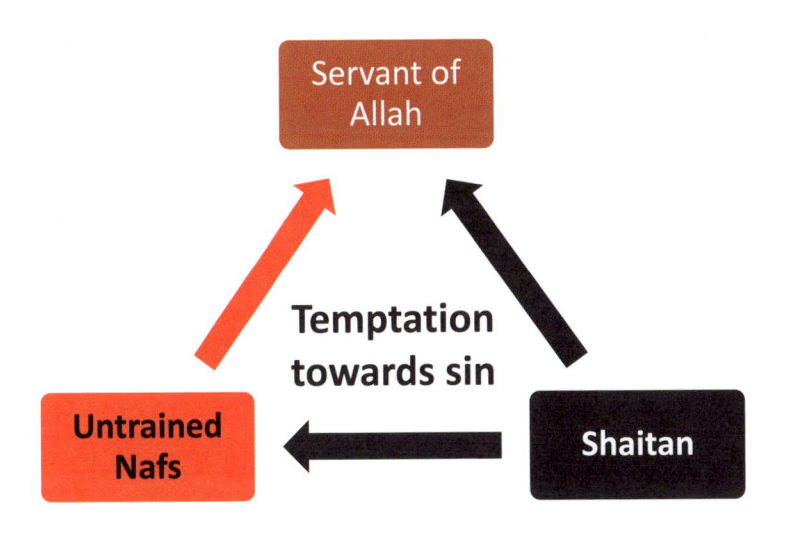

```
Servant of Allah
      ↑ ↑
Temptation towards sin
Untrained Nafs  ←  Shaitan
```

Allah will admit the righteous believers into Paradise, with running streams. The disbelievers today are enjoying themselves and eating like cattle, although the Fire is their final home. (Qur'an 47:12)

If this is the kind of lifestyle we are engaged in, we need to stop and question ourselves. Is this what Allah created us for? If it is, then why does He describe Himself as having honoured us in the Qur'an? Is this really the purpose of our life in this world?

We didn't create the Heavens and the Earth and what lies between them purposeless, though the disbelievers may think so. Woe to those who disbelieve, they will suffer in the Fire! (Qur'an 38:27)

We honoured the children of Adam and enabled them to travel across land and sea, to seek healthy sustenance and favoured them above all Our creation. (Qur'an 17:70)

I created jinn and human beings only to worship Me. (Qur'an 51:56)

What is the effect of committing sins?

The Prophet (peace be upon him) said: "Verily, when the servant commits a sin, a black mark appears upon his heart. If he abandons the sin, seeks forgiveness, and repents, then his heart will be polished. If he returns to the sin, the blackness will be increased until it overcomes his heart... (Tirmidhi)

When we commit a sin it causes our heart to darken. Indeed, the Prophet (peace be upon him) said that when we commit certain major sins the light of faith (Iman) leaves our heart. This results in us feeling distant from Allah.

The Prophet (peace be upon him) said: "The adulterer is not a believer while he is committing adultery. The drinker of wine is not a believer while he is drinking wine. The thief is not a believer while he is stealing..." (Bukhari)

Initially, we will regret what we have done because our innate nature, our conscience (the Fitrat, which we are all born with), naturally inclines towards good and is troubled when we sin.

> *The Prophet (peace be upon him) said: "...sin is what wavers in your heart and you hate for people to find out about it." (Muslim)*

However, if we don't repent (do Istighfar) and turn back to Allah, if instead we continue to follow the desires of our untrained self and whispers of the devil and persist in committing sins, the darkness shrouding our heart deepens. Eventually we reach a state where we stop being troubled by our sins. This makes it easier to continue in our bad habits and heedlessness, until we reach a stage where we begin to enjoy committing sins and actively seek out such opportunities. At such a time Allah and His Prophet are very far from our minds and we will avoid things that remind us of them. Our descent reaches its nadir when we have no shame in bragging to others of our sinful exploits and encourage or even force them to join us. Such behaviour veils us from Allah, we are floundering in the dark, completely lost.

> *Or their deeds are like veils of darkness in the deep sea covered by wave upon wave, over which clouds loom. The layers of darkness lie so densely over one another that, if one takes one's hand out of the water, one can barely see it. Anyone Allah deprives of light will have no light at all. (Qur'an 24:40)*

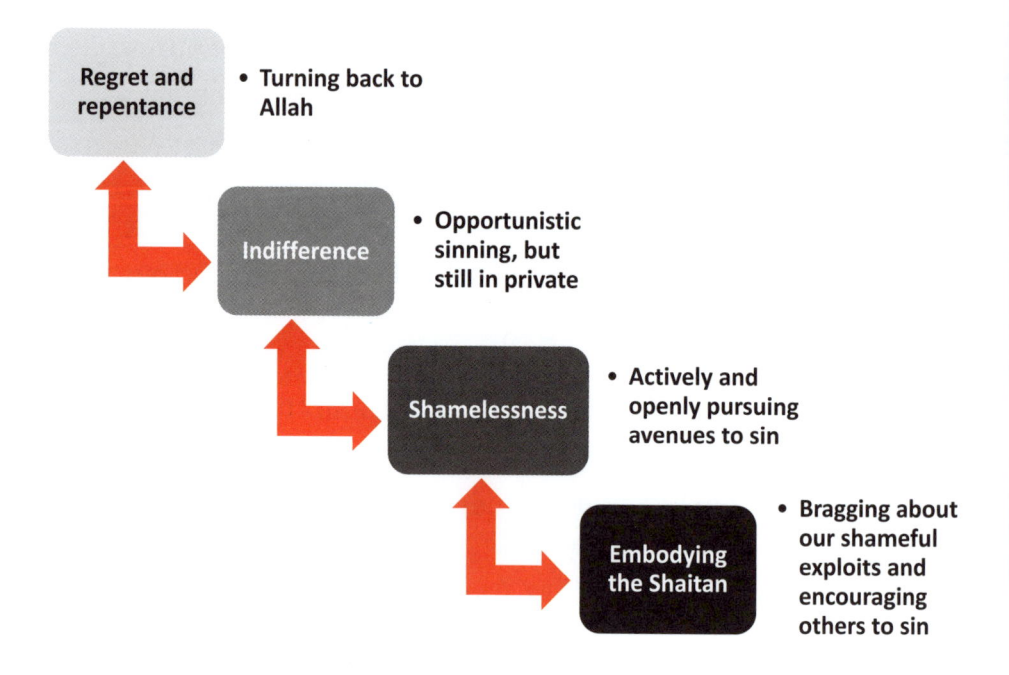

- **Regret and repentance** — Turning back to Allah
- **Indifference** — Opportunistic sinning, but still in private
- **Shamelessness** — Actively and openly pursuing avenues to sin
- **Embodying the Shaitan** — Bragging about our shameful exploits and encouraging others to sin

Food for the body, food for the soul

Our bad habits and sins, our distancing ourselves from Allah is a major cause of mental health problems such as anxiety and depression, and development of addictions such as drug and alcohol abuse, especially in the developed world. Our body is from the earth and that is what it yearns for, that is its source of sustenance and enjoyment. However, our soul (Ruh) is from the Divine realm and so that is what it yearns for, what it needs.

He created everything perfectly; He began the creation of the first human from clay, and then made his offspring from a drop of semen. Then He gave Adam his form, and blew into him of His spirit; and gave you hearing, sight and awareness. Little do you thank! (Qur'an 32:7-9)

When we deny our soul its chance to connect with the Divine, instead focussing all our energies on indulging the body, especially in ways that are Haram, we further distance our soul from the Divine and sink deeper into darkness, filling ourselves with a sense of emptiness and despair.

Misguided, we try and counter this by indulging in even more worldly pleasures, whatever they may be for us - work, entertainment, drink, drugs, spending time with friends or family, sport, gym, reading, art, shopping, travel, etc. But whatever satisfaction we gain from these is temporary and no sooner have we accomplished one goal that we are thinking about the next, because fundamentally, we remain unfulfilled.

Chasing after these fleeting highs becomes almost an addiction, but even if we were to spend our whole life achieving ever greater accomplishments and experiences, unparalleled wealth, fame and power, it would never be enough, we would still remain unsatisfied, unhappy.

> *"...those who believe, their hearts will find peace in Allah's remembrance." The fact is, hearts find peace in the remembrance of Allah! (Qur'an 13:28)*

Only when we reconnect our soul with the Divine, when we provide it with its sustenance – Dhikr'Allah (the remembrance and worship of Allah), will it be sated. And it is only then that we will find ourselves at peace and achieve a true and lasting sense of happiness that cannot be bought with all the money in the world. But to be able to do this we need to remove the barrier surrounding us, and primarily that is our own sinful habits.

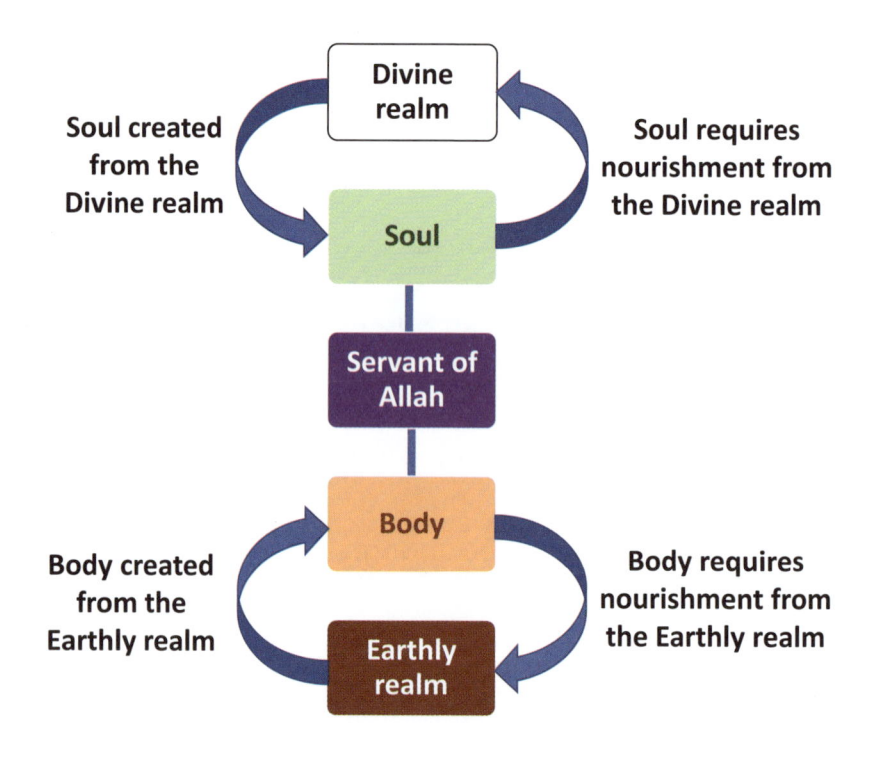

```
         ┌──── Divine ────┐
         │     realm      │
Soul created │              │ Soul requires
from the     ↓              ↓ nourishment from
Divine realm               the Divine realm
              Soul

         Servant of
           Allah

             Body
Body created ↑              ↑ Body requires
from the     │              │ nourishment from
Earthly realm│   Earthly    │ the Earthly realm
         └────  realm  ────┘
```

How to stop ourselves from committing sins

The primary method of stopping ourselves from committing sins is to increase our Taqwa – our consciousness of Allah which should change our behaviour in fear of His punishment. There are many ways we can do this.

❖ **Starting our day with the worship of Allah**

We want to make the best start to our day, so we need to ensure we get an early enough night to be able to wake for Fajr (the pre-dawn prayer).

The Prophet (peace be upon him) said: "Whoever prays Fajr is under the protection of Allah…" (Muslim)

❖ **Seeking Allah's protection**

After completing Fajr, we should raise our hands in supplication, and with the utmost sincerity ask Allah to give us a blessed day and protect us from our untrained self and the devil. One way to do this is to recite the two last Surahs of the Qur'an (Surah Al-Falaq and Surah Al-Nas) for Isti'adha (seeking protection with Allah from the unseen), as was the Sunnah of the Prophet (peace be upon him).

> Say: "I seek refuge in the Lord of the daybreak,
> from the harm of all His creation,
> from the harm of the ever-darkening night,
> from the harm of witches who blow on knots,
> and from the harm of a jealous person when jealous." (Qur'an 113)

> Say: "I seek refuge in the Lord of the people,
> the King of the people,
> the God of the people,
> from the evil of the sneaking whisperer,
> who whispers into people's hearts and minds,
> from among the jinn or the people." (Qur'an 114)

❖ Remaining in a state of Wudu

We should try and remain in a state of ablution (Wudu), as was the practice of the Awliyah-Allah (friends of Allah or saints).

> *The Prophet (peace be upon him) said: "A person in a state of Wudu is like a fasting person." (Daylami)*

Before we go to bed we should also renew our ablution so that we fall asleep in a state of ritual purity.

> *The Prophet (peace be upon him) said: "Purify these bodies, and Allah will purify you. There is not a slave who spends his night in a state of purification except that*

an Angel spends the night besides him. And whenever the slave turns over during the night, the Angel says: 'O Allah, forgive Your slave, for he went to sleep in a state of purification.'" (Tabarani)

By making a conscious decision to remain in a state of ablution throughout the day and night, a state of purity in which we worship Allah, it will make us think twice about consciously committing sins, about dirtying ourselves by disobeying and displeasing Allah.

Indeed, each time we do the ablution we should remember the saying of the Prophet (peace be upon him) that we are not only cleansing our body but also our soul.

When a believer washes his face for Wudu, all the sins that he committed with his eyes fall down with water. When he washes his hands, all the sins that he committed with his hands fall down with the last drop of water. When he washes his feet, all the sins that he committed with his feet fall down with water, with the result that he will be purified of all his [minor] sins. (Muslim)

❖ Starting every act with the name of Allah

Throughout the day we should try to keep our tongue moist with the Dhikr'Allah. We should recite the Tasmiyah/Bismillah (In the name of Allah, the Kind, the Caring) before doing anything, as the Prophet (peace be upon him) taught us to (such as work or play, eating or drinking, cooking, washing, etc.).

In reciting the name of Allah, our Creator and Sustainer, we are asking for His help with whatever it is we are about to do. Once this becomes a habit and we automatically recite the Tasmiyah before we do anything, when we find ourselves about to commit a sin, reciting the name of Allah will make us stop and think and we may be more likely to realise the mistake we are about to make.

❖ Keeping our lips moist with the remembrance of Allah

We should try and learn some of the many supplications the Prophet (peace be upon him) taught us for everyday activities, e.g.:

On waking in the morning:

> *Praise is to Allah Who gives us life after He has caused us to die and to Him is the return*

On entering the bathroom:

> *In the Name of Allah, O Allah I seek protection in You from the male and female unclean spirits*

On leaving the bathroom:

All Praise be to Allah, who removed the difficulty from me and gave me ease (relief)

On looking in a mirror:

O Allah, just as You have made my external features beautiful, make my character beautiful as well

On leaving our house:

In the Name of Allah, I have placed my trust in Allah, there is no might and no power except by Allah

On entering our house:

In the Name of Allah we enter, in the Name of Allah we leave, and upon our Lord we depend

On going to sleep:

O Allah, with your name I die and I live

This is another way in which we can keep our tongue moist with the remembrance of Allah.

❖ Anchoring our day with the Salah

It goes without saying that we need to ensure we pray the five daily prayers (Salah), ideally in the Mosque for men and at home for women (according to the Hanafi school of religious law).

These should be like anchors in our day, so that no matter what else we are doing or how busy we are, at least five times each day we return to the remembrance of Allah.

In each unit (Rak'ah) of the prayer we recite Surah Al-Fatihah (the first Surah of the Qur'an). Even if we are just performing the obligatory (Fard) parts of the prayer, this is 17 times each day. Each time we recite Surah Al-Fatihah we are asking Allah to:

> **'Guide us on the Straight Path, the Path of those You have blessed, not of those with anger on them, nor of the misguided.'**

In the Qur'an, Allah tells us that our prayer protects us from sinful and shameful behaviour:

> **Without doubt, prayer protects from indecency and evil; and to remember Allah is greater still; and Allah knows well what you do. (Qur'an 29:45)**

Syedina Ibn Abbas (may Allah be pleased with him) commentated on this verse saying,

> **"Whoever is not prohibited by his prayer from immorality and evil, then he gains nothing from his prayer but distance from Allah." (Tabari)**

❖ Making a habit of regularly fasting

Fasting is another powerful method by which we can increase our Taqwa and save ourselves from committing sins.

> *The Prophet (peace be upon him) said: "O young people! Whoever among you can marry, should marry, because it helps him lower his gaze and guard his modesty (i.e. his private parts from committing illegal sexual intercourse etc.), and whoever is not able to marry, should fast, as fasting diminishes his sexual power." (Bukhari)*

> *The Prophet (peace be upon him) said: "Fasting is a shield and a shelter against evil." (Tirmidhi)*

For more details of how fasting helps us control our untrained self, resist the whispers of the devil, and increase our consciousness of Allah, please read the chapter on fasting.

❖ Changing our environment and behaviour to remove temptations

We should optimise our environment and behaviour to minimise temptations and thereby the risk of committing sins. We should try to avoid spending excess time around members of the opposite sex (outside of what is required for education or work).

The Prophet (peace be upon him) said: "No man is alone with a woman but the Shaitan is the third one present." (Ahmad)

If such circumstances cannot be helped, we should keep our behaviour modest. We should not fall into the devil's trap of believing that our faith (Iman) is strong enough that we will be able to resist temptation. Even the Prophets of Allah (peace be upon them all), who were free from sin, prayed to Allah for His help in such circumstances (as a lesson for us).

The lady in whose house he was living tried to seduce him, bolting the doors and saying, "Come here!" "Allah forbid!" He said, "My master has given me a good home, and, in any case, wrongdoers never succeed". She lusted for him, and he would have desired her too if he hadn't seen overwhelming proof from his Lord; that was how We deflected the evil and indecency away from him. He was one of Our devoted servants. (Qur'an 12:23-24)

We should ensure our friends are a good, not bad influence on us. Allah warns us of this in the Qur'an:

Keep yourself with those who worship their Lord morning and evening, longing for His pleasure. Don't turn your eyes away from them to seek the delights of worldly life. Neither follow him whose mind is forgetful of Our remembrance, and follows his whims; his case is beyond limits. (Qur'an 18:28)

And the Prophet (peace be upon him) explained why this is so important:

The Prophet (peace be upon him) said: "The example of a good companion (who sits with you) in comparison with a bad one, is like that of the musk seller and the blacksmith's bellows (or furnace); from the first you would either buy musk or enjoy its good smell while the bellows would either burn your clothes or your house, or you get a bad nasty smell thereof." (Bukhari)

The Prophet (peace be upon him) said: "A person is likely to follow the faith of his friend, look (carefully) whom you choose to befriend." (Ahmad)

There is no denying that if we spend time with those under the control of their untrained self and the devil (e.g. people who lie or backbite regularly, make fun of Allah and His Prophets, visit clubs and bars, drink alcohol or do drugs, who have boyfriends or girlfriends and fornicate or commit adultery, commit petty and major crimes), we will find it much more difficult to control ourselves when we are in their company and they may actively encourage us to join in. Eventually, we will end up following their example.

So if need be, we need to change our circle of friends. We should choose to spend our time with those who are pious, who are trying to tread the path of closeness to Allah, thereby encouraging us to do the same.

> *The Prophet (peace be upon him) said: "Your best friend is the one who: seeing him reminds you of Allah, speaking to him increases your knowledge, and his actions remind you of the Hereafter." (Muhasibi)*

We should avoid using electronic devices in private spaces. For example, our TV or computer should not be in our bedroom or study. This also applies to using our tablet or phone. If this can't be helped we should leave the door open. All electronic devices should have robust parental controls installed. This is to reduce the temptation of looking at pornographic material, which our untrained self and the devil are more likely to tempt us to if we believe we are alone and not being watched.

❖ Finding a righteous teacher

We should visit our local Mosque and listen to the Jumu'ah Khutba (speeches given prior to the congregational prayer each Friday) and speeches given at weekly educational circles (e.g. regarding Qur'an Tafsir – explanation and commentary of the Qur'an, Seerah – biography of the Prophet, Hadith – teachings of the Prophet, Tasawwuf – working towards attaining purity of self).

We should find an Imam or another pious, religious scholar who we enjoy listening to, who we feel a natural connection to. We should attend their events, strike up a conversation with them and get to know them. We should develop a relationship, a friendship with them, and tell them how we are searching for a teacher to help us along the spiritual path to becoming a better Muslim, a better human being. If we are sincere, and they are in a position to be able to guide us, it is unlikely they will refuse.

Following that, we should keep in regular contact with them. We should do as they instruct and have the utmost respect towards them, they are our spiritual parent. Syedina Jalal'ad-Din Rumi (may Allah have mercy upon him), the renowned Persian poet and Sufi saint, told us that a moment spent in the company of the Awliyah-Allah is better than a hundred years of worship.

How to resist temptation

Even if we do all of the above, there will still be many instances each day when we feel the temptation to commit sins, especially at the start of our journey. Below, I have discussed some of the ways in which we can try to resist.

❖ Physically distancing ourselves from the temptation

When we begin to feel the temptation to disobey Allah we should try to immediately distance ourselves from whatever the source of temptation is (e.g. an attractive person flirting with us, a group of people backbiting or planning to commit a crime, an unattended object of value we feel tempted to steal, an electronic device we could access pornography on, etc.). By doing so it removes our ability to commit the sin and also gives us space to think clearly.

❖ We are never truly alone

We should remind ourselves that we are not alone. On our shoulders sit two Angels – the Kiraman Katibin ('the honourable scribes'), who are always with us.

> *When the two recording Angels, one sitting on their right and the other on their left, record. Not a word they speak goes unrecorded by a vigilant observer. (Qur'an 50:17-18)*

Imagine if we were alone in a locked, soundproof room with no cameras or windows. No-one knows where we are and no-one knows about this room. We may think that no-one could possibly find out whatever we do in such a place. But as Muslims we know this is not the case. Even in such a place the Angels on our shoulders are witnessing our every act.

Now consider the mercy of Allah in how He has instructed these Angels to record our deeds. If we intend to do a good deed, even if we don't end up carrying it out this is still recorded as one good deed because even having the intention is liked by Allah. If we actually carry out the good deed, it gets multiplied 10 to 700 times or even more when it is recorded by the Angel on the right shoulder.

In contrast to this, if we intend to commit a sin this isn't recorded because we haven't done it, we are just thinking about it. If we intend to commit a sin but stop ourselves from doing it because we remember Allah, this gets recorded as a good deed since we were going to commit a sin but stopped ourselves. If we end up committing the sin this only gets recorded as one sin by the Angel on the left.

This means that when we are tempted to commit a sin, just by being able to resist the temptation through our remembrance of Allah (the very definition of Taqwa), we are earning the blessings and pleasure of Allah more so than if we had never been tempted in the first place.

❖ Our Creator is always watching us, with us

When someone is watching us, even if it is someone we do not know, we are very careful about what we do and say. If it is a friend or relative we are even more careful, we do not want them to see us engaged in bad behaviour that is shameful. Imagine then if our mosque's Imam was with us or our Shaykh (spiritual teacher), we would be on our best behaviour.

So then consider that it is none other than Allah, the Lord of the universe, the King of kings and our Creator who is always watching us, who knows our every deed. If we truly believed this, would we be able to partake in any sinful act?

> **We created humans, and know exactly what their desires urge them to do; in fact, We are nearer to them than their jugular vein. (Qur'an 50:16)**

> **The Prophet (peace be upon him) said: "Feel shy before Allah..." (Bazzar)**

There are times when even though we believe with absolute certainty that Allah is watching us we still commit a sin because we think of it as unimportant, or minor – a small sin. We need to reflect carefully upon such behaviour. First of all, it is a grave mistake to think of any sin as minor – this is not our judgement to make. Perhaps Allah sees it as a major sin, or maybe our attitude towards it could overshadow the sin itself and lead to His anger and punishment.

Furthermore, how can we claim to love Allah if we willingly disobey Him, knowing He is watching us? One of the Awliyah-Allah said that the best Dhikr'Allah is to stop ourselves from committing a sin by reminding ourselves that Allah is watching us.

❖ The dangers of being ungrateful

Our bodies are incredible gifts from Allah for which we should be in a constant state of gratitude (Shukr). Most of our lives we take our health for granted but there are times when it becomes clear just how immense a blessing this is. We should remember the last time we were unwell, even with a minor illness such as a headache or a cold, and reflect upon how it incapacitated us from being able to study or work, or even take care of ourselves, and how we could not enjoy anything, even eating and drinking. Imagine if Allah had not blessed us with recovery and we had to spend the rest of our lives in that state? We should think about people who lose body parts such as hands or feet, arms or legs due to accidents, war, or illness, and imagine how we would cope with such a disability. What if we woke up one day and found ourselves deaf, or blind, or both?

When we use our eyes, our ears, our tongues, our hands, our feet, or our private parts to disobey Allah, this is a severe form of ingratitude. We should feel terrified doing so. Who is to say that Allah will not punish us by taking that very thing away from us?

❖ Earning Allah's pleasure

Many Muslims have a sincere desire to see the Prophet (peace be upon him) in their dreams.

> *The Prophet (peace be upon him), said: "Whoever sees me in a dream has truly seen me, for Shaitan cannot assume my form." (Bukhari)*

Similarly, travellers on the path of spiritual purity (Tasawwuf) often desire to reach a state of nearness to Allah whereupon they are granted sights from the unseen realm (Ghayb).

> *The Prophet (peace be upon him) said: Beware of the Mu'min's (believer who submits completely to the will of Allah) Firasah (spiritual insight) because he sees with the Nur (light) of Allah. (Tabarani)*

And ultimately, the only true success in this life and the next is to have pleased Allah and be rewarded with His Paradise.

> *"Allah said, 'I have prepared for My righteous slaves (such excellent things) as no eye has ever seen, no ear has ever heard, and no heart has ever perceived...'" (Muslim)*

So we should protect our eyes from seeing that which is impermissible with the sincere hope that by doing so, Allah will reward us with blessings we cannot imagine.

> *The Prophet (peace be upon him) said: "... whosoever leaves something for the sake of Allah then Allah, the Mighty and Magnificent, will replace it with something better than it." (Ahmad)*

> *The Prophet (peace be upon him) said: "The (Haram) look is a poisoned arrow from the arrows of Iblis, whoever abandons it out of fear of Allah, Allah will grant him such Iman, the sweetness of which he will experience in his heart. (Ahmad)*

Seeking forgiveness for our sins

We are all sinners – we all fall into temptation and make mistakes, this is part of what it is to be human. We are not angels (may Allah be pleased with them all) who lack free will, or the prophets (peace be upon them all) who were kept sinless through the mercy and grace of Allah. Allah knows this, He is the one who created us. In Arabic a human being is called an 'Insan' – which comes from the verb Nasiyah, meaning to forget.

> *The Prophet (peace be upon him) said: "By Him in whose hand is my soul, if you did not sin, Allah would replace you with people who would sin and they would seek forgiveness from Allah and he would forgive them." (Muslim)*

This does not mean that Allah wants us to commit sins but that given it is impossible for us to be completely sin free, whenever we become heedless and disobey Him, Allah wants us to realise our mistake and turn to Him in repentance.

> **Whoever does an evil deed or wrongs himself but then seeks Allah's forgiveness, he will find Allah Forgiving, Kind. (Qur'an 4:110)**

The degree to which Allah delights at our repentance is exemplified by the following Hadith:

> **The Prophet (peace be upon him) said: "Verily, Allah is more pleased with the repentance of His slave than a person who has his camel in a waterless desert carrying his provision of food and drink and it is lost. He, having lost all hopes (to get that back), lies down in shade and is disappointed about his camel; when all of a sudden he finds that camel standing before him. He takes hold of its reins and then out of boundless joy blurts out: 'O Allah, You are my slave and I am Your Rabb.' He commits this mistake out of extreme joy." (Muslim)**

This is why we should not hesitate to repent whenever we give in to our temptations — it is a way for us to draw closer to Allah. But our repentance needs to be sincere, which means being truly ashamed of ourselves and our actions and to make the firm intention to never commit that sin again, with the help of

Allah. When we do this Allah is The Forgiving (Al Gaffur), The Pardoner (Al Afuw), not only is the sin forgiven it is as if it was never committed in the first place.

> *Say: "My servants who wronged themselves, don't be hopeless of Allah's Kindness; Allah forgives all the sins, He is the Forgiver, the Kind." (Qur'an 39:53)*

> *The Prophet (peace be upon him) said: "A believer will be brought close to his Rabb [Lord] on the Day of Resurrection and, enveloping him in His Mercy, Allah will make him confess his sins by saying: `Do you remember (doing) this sin and this sin?' He will reply: `My Rabb, I remember.' Then Allah will say: `I covered it up for you in the life of world, and I forgive it for you today.' Then the record of his good deeds will be handed to him." (Bukhari)*

But even if our repentance is sincere, i.e. we make a firm intention to never commit that sin again, most of us will.

> *The Prophet (peace be upon him), said: "There is no believing servant but that he has a sin he habitually commits from time to time, or a sin abiding over him that he does not abandon until he departs the world. Verily, the believer was created to be tested, repenting and forgetful. If he is reminded, he will remember." (Tabarani)*

When this happens the devil tells us that we should feel ashamed of ourselves for asking Allah to forgive us again and again when we carry on committing the same sin over and over again, that this is making a mockery of Allah's forgiveness, that He will not forgive us and in fact we will be earning His anger.

This is not true. It is a powerful lie of the 'Great Deceiver' (Shaitan), it is his way of stopping us from being forgiven for our sins. He is trying to make us follow his example when not only did he refuse to prostrate to Syedina Adam (peace be upon him) but tried to justify his disobedience and blamed Allah for leading him astray, for which he was cursed for all eternity and expelled from the Heavens. He does not want us to follow the example of Syedina Adam and Syedatuna Hawwa (peace be upon them both) who repented as soon as they realised their disobedience to Allah in eating from the forbidden tree.

The truth is that Allah knows that we are forgetful, we are weak, we give in to our temptations, and so as long as our repentance is sincere His mercy and love for us is such that He is not only willing to forgive us again and again but this is a means to earn His pleasure and draw closer to Him.

> *"Allah the Exalted said: 'O son of Adam, if you call upon me and place your hope in me, I will forgive you without any reservation. O son of Adam, if you have sins piling up to the clouds and then ask for my forgiveness, I will forgive you without any reservation. O son of Adam, if you come to me with enough sins to fill the earth and you meet*

me without associating a partner with me, I will come to you with enough forgiveness to fill the earth.'" (Tirmidhi)

Summary

I have talked about our two arch-nemeses (the untrained self and the devil) who encourage us to indulge ourselves and commit sins. The primary method of resisting temptation and training our Nafs is to increase our Taqwa – our consciousness of Allah that should change our behaviour in fear of His punishment.

I have discussed different ways we can do this, including starting our day with Allah's worship and seeking His protection, remaining in a state of ablution, starting every act with Allah's name and keeping our lips moist with His remembrance throughout the day, regularly fasting, changing our environment and behaviour, and seeking the company and guidance of a righteous teacher.

We should physically distance ourselves from the source of temptation, and also remember that we are never truly alone; the Kiraman Katibin record our every deed and furthermore our Creator is always watching us. We should remind ourselves of the ingratitude we display to Allah when we disobey him using the immense blessings He has showered upon us, and feel terrified of His taking them away. Alternatively, if we resist temptation and give up something for the sake of Allah, this is a means of earning His pleasure and He will surely reward us and replace it with something better.

Finally, I have stressed the importance of seeking sincere forgiveness, since despite striving to purify ourselves we are all sinners and will inevitably give in to temptation at times, especially if we already have bad habits. Regular Istighfar removes the stain of sins from our soul and draws us closer to Allah. This is the connection with the Divine that our soul yearns for; the only thing that can bring peace to our heart.

Striving for purity of self

> *You who have Iman! Have Taqwa of Allah and let each self look to what it has sent forward for tomorrow...* (Qur'an 59:18)

> *Syedina Umar (may Allah be pleased with him) said: "Call yourselves to account before you are called to account, and weigh yourselves before you are weighed, as calling yourselves to account today will make it easier for you when you are called to account tomorrow, and be adorned for the great appearance: that Day shall you be brought to Judgement, and not a secret of yours will be hidden." (Ahmad)*

Following Allah's guidance and the practice of His Prophets and friends, we should make it a habit to reflect upon how we have spent our time each day before going to sleep. We should rejoice at the good deeds we have done by the grace of Allah and thank Him for His countless blessings upon us, and feel ashamed of the sins we committed and sincerely repent for them. We should think about how we will try and avoid these sins in future and pray to Allah for help. We should have this noble intention while remembering the Hadith Qudsi:

> *"He who draws close to Me a hand's span, I will draw close to him an arm's length. And whoever draws near Me an arm's length, I will draw near him a fathom's length. And whoever comes to Me walking, I will go to him running..." (Bukhari)*

To help us do this and establish such a habit, on the following pages I have included tables to be completed for each day, concentrating on a single sin or bad habit. We need to avoid the trap that the devil will set for us; to feel overly guilty about giving into temptation and committing sins, to the extent that we do not seek repentance out of a misplaced sense of shame and loss of hope in Allah's mercy. We also need to avoid the other extreme, to commit a sin knowing it is wrong and to repent knowing we are not going to give it up. The only person we are lying to is ourselves.

Date:	
Which sin did I commit today?	
What factors contributed to this happening?	
How did I feel after realising my mistake?	
Did I sincerely repent?	Yes / No
If not, why not?	
How will I avoid committing this sin in future	

Date:	
Which sin did I commit today?	
What factors contributed to this happening?	
How did I feel after realising my mistake?	
Did I sincerely repent?	Yes / No
If not, why not?	
How will I avoid committing this sin in future	

Purity of Self: Avoiding the stain of sins

Date:	
Which sin did I commit today?	
What factors contributed to this happening?	
How did I feel after realising my mistake?	
Did I sincerely repent?	Yes / No
If not, why not?	
How will I avoid committing this sin in future	

Date:	
Which sin did I commit today?	
What factors contributed to this happening?	
How did I feel after realising my mistake?	
Did I sincerely repent?	Yes / No
If not, why not?	
How will I avoid committing this sin in future	

Date:	
Which sin did I commit today?	
What factors contributed to this happening?	
How did I feel after realising my mistake?	
Did I sincerely repent?	Yes / No
If not, why not?	
How will I avoid committing this sin in future	

Date:	
Which sin did I commit today?	
What factors contributed to this happening?	
How did I feel after realising my mistake?	
Did I sincerely repent?	Yes / No
If not, why not?	
How will I avoid committing this sin in future	

Purity of Self: Avoiding the stain of sins

Date:	
Which sin did I commit today?	
What factors contributed to this happening?	
How did I feel after realising my mistake?	
Did I sincerely repent?	Yes / No
If not, why not?	
How will I avoid committing this sin in future	

Date:	
Which sin did I commit today?	
What factors contributed to this happening?	
How did I feel after realising my mistake?	
Did I sincerely repent?	Yes / No
If not, why not?	
How will I avoid committing this sin in future	

Date:	
Which sin did I commit today?	
What factors contributed to this happening?	
How did I feel after realising my mistake?	
Did I sincerely repent?	Yes / No
If not, why not?	
How will I avoid committing this sin in future	

Date:	
Which sin did I commit today?	
What factors contributed to this happening?	
How did I feel after realising my mistake?	
Did I sincerely repent?	Yes / No
If not, why not?	
How will I avoid committing this sin in future	

Purity of Self: Avoiding the stain of sins

Date:	
Which sin did I commit today?	
What factors contributed to this happening?	
How did I feel after realising my mistake?	
Did I sincerely repent?	Yes / No
If not, why not?	
How will I avoid committing this sin in future	

Date:	
Which sin did I commit today?	
What factors contributed to this happening?	
How did I feel after realising my mistake?	
Did I sincerely repent?	Yes / No
If not, why not?	
How will I avoid committing this sin in future	

Date:	
Which sin did I commit today?	
What factors contributed to this happening?	
How did I feel after realising my mistake?	
Did I sincerely repent?	Yes / No
If not, why not?	
How will I avoid committing this sin in future	

Date:	
Which sin did I commit today?	
What factors contributed to this happening?	
How did I feel after realising my mistake?	
Did I sincerely repent?	Yes / No
If not, why not?	
How will I avoid committing this sin in future	

Purity of Self: Avoiding the stain of sins

Date:	
Which sin did I commit today?	
What factors contributed to this happening?	
How did I feel after realising my mistake?	
Did I sincerely repent?	Yes / No
If not, why not?	
How will I avoid committing this sin in future	

Date:	
Which sin did I commit today?	
What factors contributed to this happening?	
How did I feel after realising my mistake?	
Did I sincerely repent?	Yes / No
If not, why not?	
How will I avoid committing this sin in future	

Date:	
Which sin did I commit today?	
What factors contributed to this happening?	
How did I feel after realising my mistake?	
Did I sincerely repent?	Yes / No
If not, why not?	
How will I avoid committing this sin in future	

Date:	
Which sin did I commit today?	
What factors contributed to this happening?	
How did I feel after realising my mistake?	
Did I sincerely repent?	Yes / No
If not, why not?	
How will I avoid committing this sin in future	

Purity of Self: Avoiding the stain of sins

Date:	
Which sin did I commit today?	
What factors contributed to this happening?	
How did I feel after realising my mistake?	
Did I sincerely repent?	Yes / No
If not, why not?	
How will I avoid committing this sin in future	

Date:	
Which sin did I commit today?	
What factors contributed to this happening?	
How did I feel after realising my mistake?	
Did I sincerely repent?	Yes / No
If not, why not?	
How will I avoid committing this sin in future	

Date:	
Which sin did I commit today?	
What factors contributed to this happening?	
How did I feel after realising my mistake?	
Did I sincerely repent?	Yes / No
If not, why not?	
How will I avoid committing this sin in future	

Date:	
Which sin did I commit today?	
What factors contributed to this happening?	
How did I feel after realising my mistake?	
Did I sincerely repent?	Yes / No
If not, why not?	
How will I avoid committing this sin in future	

Purity of Self: Avoiding the stain of sins

Date:	
Which sin did I commit today?	
What factors contributed to this happening?	
How did I feel after realising my mistake?	
Did I sincerely repent?	Yes / No
If not, why not?	
How will I avoid committing this sin in future	

Date:	
Which sin did I commit today?	
What factors contributed to this happening?	
How did I feel after realising my mistake?	
Did I sincerely repent?	Yes / No
If not, why not?	
How will I avoid committing this sin in future	

Date:	
Which sin did I commit today?	
What factors contributed to this happening?	
How did I feel after realising my mistake?	

Did I sincerely repent?	Yes / No
If not, why not?	
How will I avoid committing this sin in future	

Date:	
Which sin did I commit today?	
What factors contributed to this happening?	
How did I feel after realising my mistake?	

Did I sincerely repent?	Yes / No
If not, why not?	
How will I avoid committing this sin in future	

Purity of Self: Avoiding the stain of sins

Date:	
Which sin did I commit today?	
What factors contributed to this happening?	
How did I feel after realising my mistake?	
Did I sincerely repent?	Yes / No
If not, why not?	
How will I avoid committing this sin in future	

Date:	
Which sin did I commit today?	
What factors contributed to this happening?	
How did I feel after realising my mistake?	
Did I sincerely repent?	Yes / No
If not, why not?	
How will I avoid committing this sin in future	

Date:	
Which sin did I commit today?	
What factors contributed to this happening?	
How did I feel after realising my mistake?	
Did I sincerely repent?	Yes / No
If not, why not?	
How will I avoid committing this sin in future	

Date:	
Which sin did I commit today?	
What factors contributed to this happening?	
How did I feel after realising my mistake?	
Did I sincerely repent?	Yes / No
If not, why not?	
How will I avoid committing this sin in future	

Purity of Self: Avoiding the stain of sins

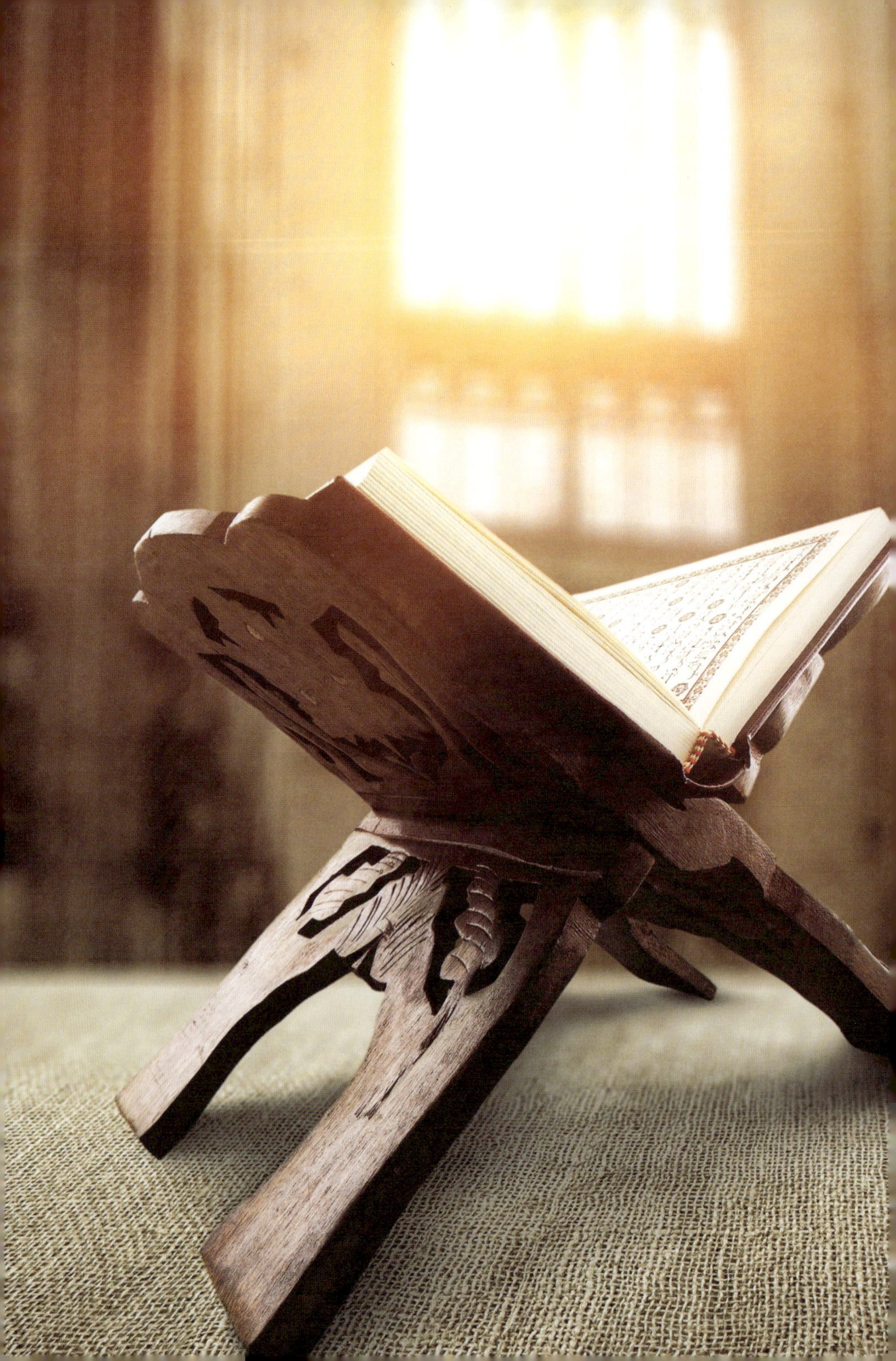

The Qur'an: Reciting, understanding, and internalising it

Islam – the universal religion from the beginning of time

Islam ('submission to the will of Allah') is the true religion of all Prophets, from the Prophet Adam to the Prophet Muhammad (peace be upon them all). As human society developed over time so did their relationship with their Creator, until the final Messenger, the 'Seal of the Prophets' (peace be upon him) was sent with the perfected religion:

> *Today, I have completed your religion for you; I gave My favour in full, and I am pleased that Islam is your religion. (Qur'an 5:3)*

Different revelations with different prophets for different people

The purpose of the Prophet was to guide mankind upon Sirat'al-Mustaqeem ('the straight path') and many of them were sent with Revelation, e.g. Gospel (Injil) of the Prophet Isa, Torah (Tawrah) of the Prophet Musa, Psalms (Zabur) of the Prophet Dawud (peace be upon them all), and many more which have been lost over the ages.

The final Prophet, Muhammad (peace be upon him) was given the final Revelation, the Qur'an, over a period of 23 years:

> *This Quran could not have been invented independently of Allah; rather it confirms what came before it and is an explanation of that Book in which there is no doubt, which is from the Lord of the Universe. (Qur'an 10:37)*

The Qur'an was preserved by the oral and written tradition

When verses of the Qur'an were revealed, the Prophet (peace be upon him) recited them to his Sahabah (companions – may Allah be pleased with them all) and instructed them where the verses fit in relation to others. Many companions had memorised either parts or all of the Qur'an. The literate ones would also write it down on cleaned pieces of bone, leather, or leaves, which were carefully stored. During the caliphate of Syedina Abu-Bakr (may Allah be pleased with him) the written Qur'an was compiled in the form of the book we have today (called the Mus'haf).

The Qur'an cannot be corrupted

The previous revelations were changed by misguided people:

> *Do you expect them to believe you when a group of them hears the words of Allah and, after understanding them, deliberately changes them? (Qur'an 2:75)*

> *Some of them twist their tongues when reciting from the Book to make you think it is from the Book, even though it forms no part of the Book, and they say: "This is from Allah," even though it is not from Allah, and they knowingly tell lies against Allah. (Qur'an 3:78)*

However, Allah has taken it upon Himself to safeguard the Qur'an:

> *We revealed the Reminder, and We are its Protectors. (Qur'an 15:9)*

The Qur'an we have today, more than 1400 years after the time of the Prophet (peace be upon him), is identical to the very oldest copies of the written Qur'an that have been found from the time of the first and second-generation Muslims (may Allah be pleased with them all).

The significance of the Holy Qur'an

What does Allah, Himself, say about His Qur'an?

This is the Majestic book, there is no doubt in it, a guidance for the pious (Qur'an 2:2)

People, your Lord's teachings have come to you; they're a healing balm for the diseases of the heart, guidance and beneficial teachings for the believers. (Qur'an 10:57)

This is a Book that We sent down to you, a blessed Book, so people might think about its message, and the intelligent might pay attention. (Qur'an 38:29)

He reveals clear teachings to His servant, to take you out of darkness into light, and treats you kindly. (Qur'an 57:9)

These verses show that Allah revealed the Qur'an for us to reflect upon and understand, to achieve guidance and salvation.

The Prophet Muhammad (peace be upon him) said, "Indeed this Qur'an is a rope – one end of it is in the hand of Allah and the other end is in your hands. So, hold firmly to it [the result would be] that you would never go astray and never be destroyed [no matter what the circumstance]." (Ibn Hibban)

The Prophet Muhammad (peace be upon him) said, "The Qur'an is an intercessor and its intercession is accepted and its plea is believed. Whoever makes it lead him – it leads him to Paradise and whomsoever places it behind him [the result will be] he is dragged to the Fire." (Ibn Hibban)

The greatest miracle of the Prophet - the speech of Allah

Indeed, the Qur'an is the greatest miracle that Allah gave to His final Prophet (peace be upon him):

"Every Prophet was given a miracle, the type of which brings mankind to faith. What I was given is a revelation that Allah sent down to me…" (Muslim)

To truly understand the nature of this miracle we need to realise what it is. The Qur'an is literally the speech of Allah, transmitted in the form of Revelation. It descended upon the heart of the Prophet (peace be upon him), and through him to the rest of mankind, during his lifetime and until the Day of Judgement.

Therefore, as Allah's speech, the Qur'an is not something that can be separated from His essence (similar to the other 'Siffat' or attributes of Allah), and as such is also infinite and uncreated.

> *The Prophet Muhammad (peace be upon him) said, "The superiority of the Speech of Allah compared to all other speech is like the superiority of Allah over His creation." (Tirmidhi)*

The tremendousness of this fact is truly profound. Allah has given us something that is Divine, and therefore unique, unlike anything else in this Universe.

> *Say: "If all humanity and jinn got together to bring a book like this Quran, they wouldn't be able to bring it, no matter how much they helped each other." (Qur'an 17:88)*

> *Had We revealed this Quran on a mountain, you would have seen it humble itself and turn to dust out of fear of Allah. We give these examples so people may reflect. (Qur'an 59:21)*

When we understand this then it is easy to see why reciting, understanding and acting upon the Qur'an is the greatest form of Dhikr'Allah that we have.

> *The Prophet Muhammad (peace be upon him) said, "You will not come back to Allah with anything better than that which came from Him (i.e. the Qur'an)." (Al Hakim)*

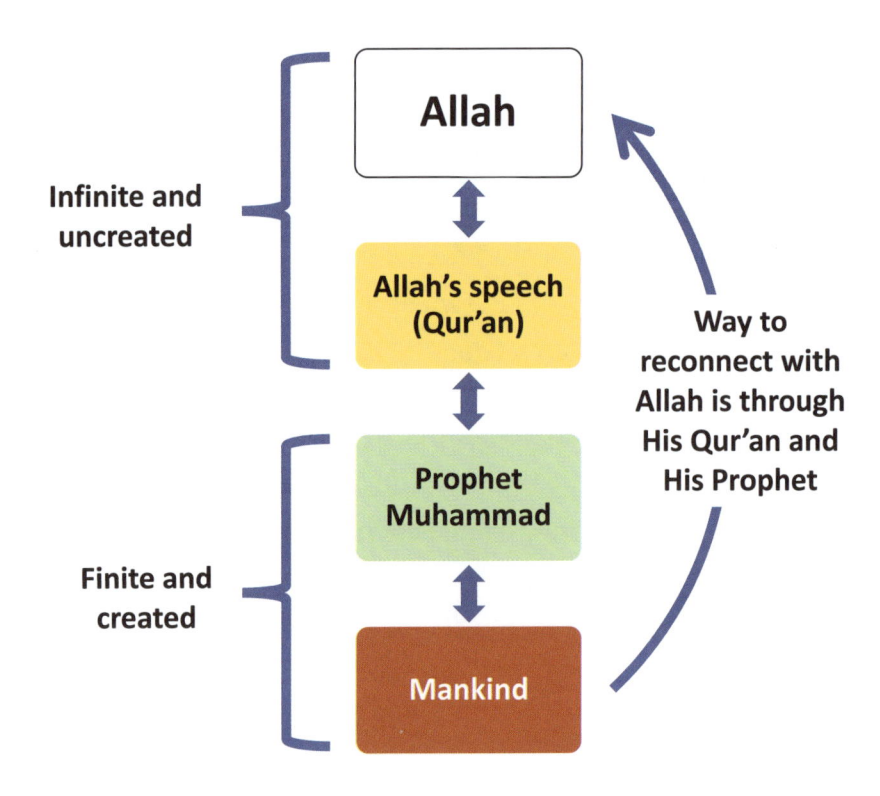

```
Infinite and      ⎧  ┌─────────────┐
uncreated         ⎨  │    Allah    │◄──┐
                  ⎩  └──────┬──────┘   │
                            ↕          │
                     ┌─────────────┐   │  Way to
                     │Allah's speech│  │  reconnect with
                     │   (Qur'an)  │   │  Allah is through
                     └──────┬──────┘   │  His Qur'an and
                            ↕          │  His Prophet
Finite and        ⎧  ┌─────────────┐   │
created           ⎨  │   Prophet   │   │
                  ⎨  │  Muhammad   │   │
                  ⎨  └──────┬──────┘   │
                  ⎨         ↕          │
                  ⎨  ┌─────────────┐   │
                  ⎩  │   Mankind   │───┘
                     └─────────────┘
```

A bottomless well of guidance

In the same way that Allah has no beginning and no end (i.e. He is infinite), so too is His word. Since the time of the Prophet (peace be upon him), scholars have spent their lives studying the Qur'an, and written countless books of Tafsir (commentary and explanation of the Qur'an). Despite its revelation over 1400 years ago, it is not an ancient text. Each generation of scholars continues to derive guidance from it which is relevant to the changing world around us.

> "...We revealed to you a glorious Book that explains the truth about all things; it is guidance, a kindness and good news for the Muslims (Qur'an 16:89)

What relationship should we have with the Qur'an?

The Qur'an should be the most important thing in our lives. Allah has given us a miracle which holds the secrets to this life and the next, and the key to purifying our outward and inward character and attaining His nearness. So, we must not only recite the Arabic but study its translation and commentary with our learned teachers, and internalise and act upon what we learn. It is not enough for us to keep the written Qur'an on a high shelf in our house never to be opened, although indeed, even that is a source of blessing.

> *Syedina Abdullah ibn Masud (may Allah be pleased with him)* said, "When a man amongst us learned ten verses [of the Qur'an], he would not move on [to the next verses] until he had understood their meanings and how to act by them." (Tabari)

When the Prophet (peace be upon him) used to recite the Qur'an it was as if he was having a conversation with Allah:

> *"And when he (peace be upon him) recited the verses which referred to the glory of Allah, he glorified Him, The Great, and when he recited the verses that mention supplication, he supplicated, and when he recited the verses that mention seeking refuge of the Rabb [Lord], he sought (His) refuge."* (Muslim)

The famous saint, Muhyi'ad-Din Ibn al-Arabi of Andalusia (may Allah have mercy upon him) attributed everything he knew to reciting the Qur'an. He spent hours each day alone with Allah in this way; 'he read it as a lover would read a letter from an absent beloved.'

He would recite the Qur'an in the way of the Prophet (peace be upon him) and left advice for us:

> *"Read the Qur'an slowly. When a verse asks a question, reply to it, when a verse reminds, heed its reminder, when a verse gives an instruction, follow it. When told to seek God's protection, recite 'I seek Allah's protection' where it asks you to seek forgiveness, seek forgiveness. When you find the qualities of God-fearing people, ask yourself which of these do I possess and which do I need to develop? Be thankful to Allah for those you have and strive to achieve those you lack. Similarly, when you come across*

verses describing the disbelievers, examine yourself, do you have any of these traits? If you do, then rid yourself of them. This is the best way to recite the Qur'an."

The countless blessings attained by engaging with the Qur'an

Apart from the ultimate benefit of guidance that we derive from the Qur'an, Allah has also hidden countless other blessings within recitation of His word, and within specific verses of which only a few examples are given below.

> *The Prophet (peace be upon him) said, "Whoever recites one letter from the Book of Allah then he will receive a good reward, and every good deed is rewarded with ten times its like. I do not say that 'Alif Laam Meem' is one word but 'Alif' is one word, 'Laam' is one word and 'Meem' is one word." (Tirmidhi)*

Regarding Surah Al-Fatihah (Qur'an 1), and the last two verses of Surah Al-Baqarah (Qur'an 2:285-286):

> *Syedina Ibn Abbas (may Allah be pleased with him) narrated, "While Jibra'il was with the Prophet (peace be upon him), he heard a noise from above. Jibra'il lifted his sight to the sky and said: "This is a door in the Heavens*

being opened, and it has never been opened before now." An Angel descended from that door and came to the Prophet (peace be upon him) and said: "Receive the glad tidings of two lights that you have been given, which no other Prophet before you was given: the Opening of the Book (Al-Fatiha), and the last verses of 'al-Baqarah.' You will not read a letter of them except that you will gain its benefit." (Muslim)

Regarding Ayat'al-Kursi' (Qur'an 2:255):

The Prophet (peace be upon him) said "Whoever recites Ayat'al-Kursi'after every obligatory prayer, then there is nothing between him and his entrance into Paradise except his death." (Al-Nasai)

Regarding Surah Al-Yaseen (Qur'an 36):

Syedina Ibn Abbas (may Allah be pleased with him) narrated, "Whoever recites Yaseen in the morning, his work for that entire day will be made easy and whoever recites it at the end of the day, his tasks until the next morning will be made easy." (al-Darimi)

Regarding Surah Al-Ikhlas (Qur'an 112):

The Prophet (peace be upon him) said, 'By Him in Whose hand my soul is, it [Surah Al-Ikhlas] is equal to one third of the Quran." (Bukhari)

Regarding Surah Al-Falaq and Al-Nas (Qur'an 113-114):

"The Messenger of Allah (peace be upon him) used to seek refuge with Allah from the Jinn and from the evil eye until the Mu'wadaitain (Surah Al-Falaq and Al-Nas) were revealed, and when they were revealed He started to recite them and not anything else." (Tirmidhi)

Developing a habit of reciting, understanding, and acting upon the Qur'an

The purpose of this chapter is to provide a practical means of developing a relationship with the word of Allah. The aim is to recite some Qur'an every day, with translation, so we can understand what we have read, and from this to find a message or instruction to act upon. All of this should be recorded on the following pages to help develop this habit.

We need to avoid the trap that the devil will set for us; if we try to recite too much in one go we will find it difficult to do this daily, being more likely to abandon the habit before it becomes established. Instead, we should start small and gradually increase, remembering the teaching of our Prophet (peace be upon him):

"Take up good deeds only as much as you are able, for the best deeds are those done regularly even if they are few." (Ibn Majah)

In this way, reciting, understanding, and acting upon the Qur'an will become easy for us and part of our daily routine. We should have this noble intention from the very beginning and supplicate to Allah to help us in this struggle. As we are told in the Hadith Qudsi:

"He who draws close to Me a hand's span, I will draw close to him an arm's length. And whoever draws near Me an arm's length, I will draw near him a fathom's length. And whoever comes to Me walking, I will go to him running..." (Bukhari)

The Qur'an: Reciting, understanding, and internalising it

Date:	
Did I recite the Qur'an today?	Yes / No
How much did I read (pages/chapters)?	
Did I read it with translation/commentary?	Yes / No
What message did I take from what I read?	

Date:	
Did I recite the Qur'an today?	Yes / No
How much did I read (pages/chapters)?	
Did I read it with translation/commentary?	Yes / No
What message did I take from what I read?	

Drawing closer to Allah and His Prophet A Practical Guide

Date:	
Did I recite the Qur'an today?	Yes / No
How much did I read (pages/chapters)?	
Did I read it with translation/commentary?	Yes / No
What message did I take from what I read?	

Date:	
Did I recite the Qur'an today?	Yes / No
How much did I read (pages/chapters)?	
Did I read it with translation/commentary?	Yes / No
What message did I take from what I read?	

The Qur'an: Reciting, understanding, and internalising it

Date:	
Did I recite the Qur'an today?	Yes / No
How much did I read (pages/chapters)?	
Did I read it with translation/commentary?	Yes / No
What message did I take from what I read?	

Date:	
Did I recite the Qur'an today?	Yes / No
How much did I read (pages/chapters)?	
Did I read it with translation/commentary?	Yes / No
What message did I take from what I read?	

Date:	
Did I recite the Qur'an today?	Yes / No
How much did I read (pages/chapters)?	
Did I read it with translation/commentary?	Yes / No
What message did I take from what I read?	

Date:	
Did I recite the Qur'an today?	Yes / No
How much did I read (pages/chapters)?	
Did I read it with translation/commentary?	Yes / No
What message did I take from what I read?	

The Qur'an: Reciting, understanding, and internalising it

Date:	
Did I recite the Qur'an today?	Yes / No
How much did I read (pages/chapters)?	
Did I read it with translation/commentary?	Yes / No
What message did I take from what I read?	

Date:	
Did I recite the Qur'an today?	Yes / No
How much did I read (pages/chapters)?	
Did I read it with translation/commentary?	Yes / No
What message did I take from what I read?	

Date:	
Did I recite the Qur'an today?	Yes / No
How much did I read (pages/chapters)?	
Did I read it with translation/commentary?	Yes / No
What message did I take from what I read?	

Date:	
Did I recite the Qur'an today?	Yes / No
How much did I read (pages/chapters)?	
Did I read it with translation/commentary?	Yes / No
What message did I take from what I read?	

The Qur'an: Reciting, understanding, and internalising it

Date:	
Did I recite the Qur'an today?	Yes / No
How much did I read (pages/chapters)?	
Did I read it with translation/commentary?	Yes / No
What message did I take from what I read?	

Date:	
Did I recite the Qur'an today?	Yes / No
How much did I read (pages/chapters)?	
Did I read it with translation/commentary?	Yes / No
What message did I take from what I read?	

Date:	
Did I recite the Qur'an today?	Yes / No
How much did I read (pages/chapters)?	
Did I read it with translation/commentary?	Yes / No
What message did I take from what I read?	

Date:	
Did I recite the Qur'an today?	Yes / No
How much did I read (pages/chapters)?	
Did I read it with translation/commentary?	Yes / No
What message did I take from what I read?	

The Qur'an: Reciting, understanding, and internalising it

Date:	
Did I recite the Qur'an today?	Yes / No
How much did I read (pages/chapters)?	
Did I read it with translation/commentary?	Yes / No
What message did I take from what I read?	

Date:	
Did I recite the Qur'an today?	Yes / No
How much did I read (pages/chapters)?	
Did I read it with translation/commentary?	Yes / No
What message did I take from what I read?	

Date:	
Did I recite the Qur'an today?	Yes / No
How much did I read (pages/chapters)?	
Did I read it with translation/commentary?	Yes / No
What message did I take from what I read?	

Date:	
Did I recite the Qur'an today?	Yes / No
How much did I read (pages/chapters)?	
Did I read it with translation/commentary?	Yes / No
What message did I take from what I read?	

The Qur'an: Reciting, understanding, and internalising it

Date:	
Did I recite the Qur'an today?	Yes / No
How much did I read (pages/chapters)?	
Did I read it with translation/commentary?	Yes / No
What message did I take from what I read?	

Date:	
Did I recite the Qur'an today?	Yes / No
How much did I read (pages/chapters)?	
Did I read it with translation/commentary?	Yes / No
What message did I take from what I read?	

Date:	
Did I recite the Qur'an today?	Yes / No
How much did I read (pages/chapters)?	
Did I read it with translation/commentary?	Yes / No
What message did I take from what I read?	

Date:	
Did I recite the Qur'an today?	Yes / No
How much did I read (pages/chapters)?	
Did I read it with translation/commentary?	Yes / No
What message did I take from what I read?	

The Qur'an: Reciting, understanding, and internalising it

Date:	
Did I recite the Qur'an today?	Yes / No
How much did I read (pages/chapters)?	
Did I read it with translation/commentary?	Yes / No
What message did I take from what I read?	

Date:	
Did I recite the Qur'an today?	Yes / No
How much did I read (pages/chapters)?	
Did I read it with translation/commentary?	Yes / No
What message did I take from what I read?	

Date:	
Did I recite the Qur'an today?	Yes / No
How much did I read (pages/chapters)?	
Did I read it with translation/commentary?	Yes / No
What message did I take from what I read?	

Date:	
Did I recite the Qur'an today?	Yes / No
How much did I read (pages/chapters)?	
Did I read it with translation/commentary?	Yes / No
What message did I take from what I read?	

The Qur'an: Reciting, understanding, and internalising it

Date:	
Did I recite the Qur'an today?	Yes / No
How much did I read (pages/chapters)?	
Did I read it with translation/commentary?	Yes / No
What message did I take from what I read?	

Date:	
Did I recite the Qur'an today?	Yes / No
How much did I read (pages/chapters)?	
Did I read it with translation/commentary?	Yes / No
What message did I take from what I read?	

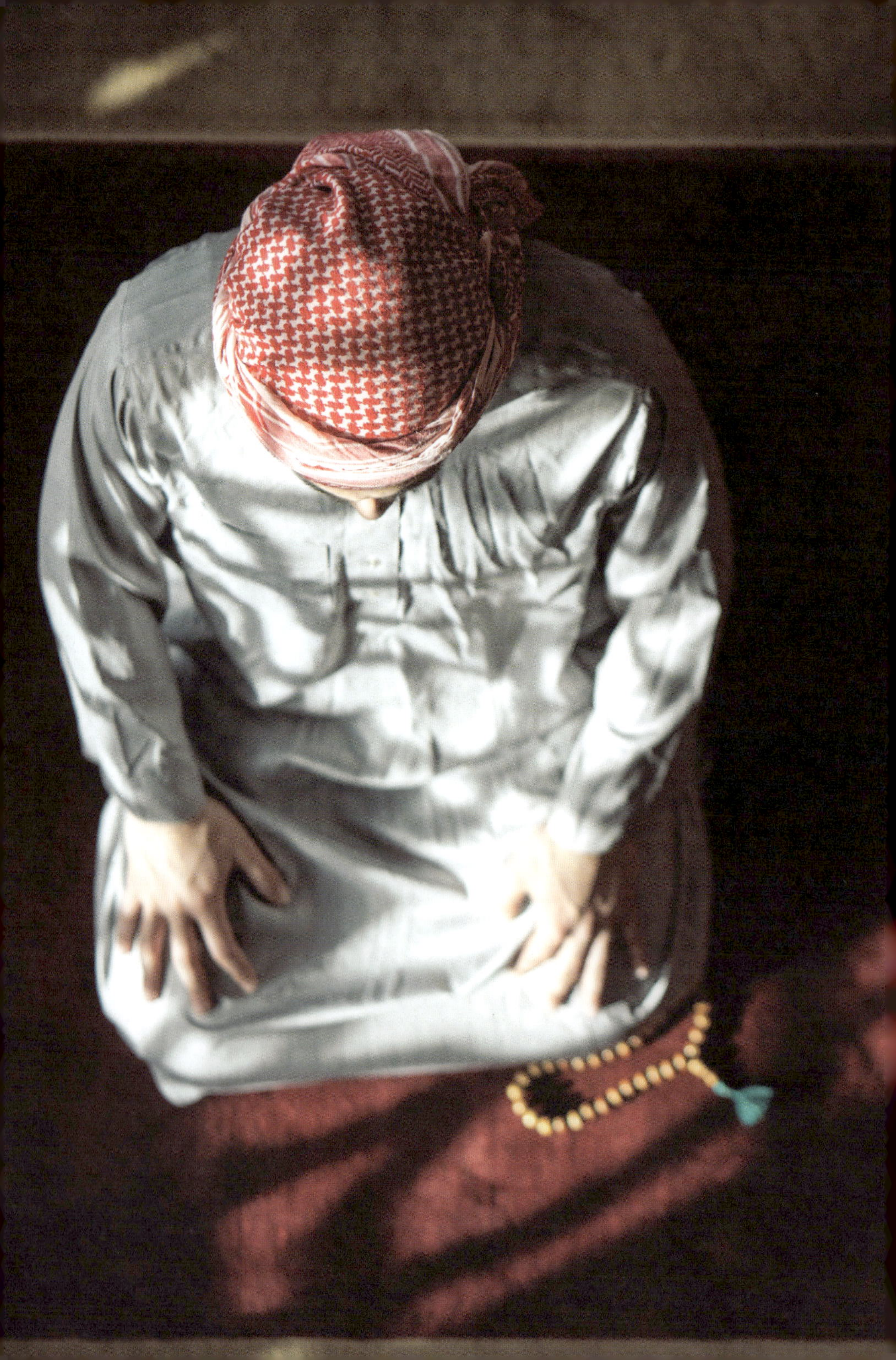

The Salah:
Praying with Khushu

There is no Islam without Salah

The five daily prayers (Salah) are one of the five pillars of Islam. As such they are obligatory for all Muslims. This has been made very clear to us in the Qur'an and Hadith:

> I am Allah. There is no god but Me, so worship Me. Perform the prayer to remember Me. (Qur'an 20:14)

> Perform prayer, pay Zakat, and bow down with those who bow in prayer. (Qur'an 2:43)

> The Prophet (peace be upon him) said, "The first action for which a servant of Allah will be held accountable on the Day of Resurrection will be his Prayers. If they are in order, then he will have prospered and succeeded. If they are lacking, then he will have failed and lost..." (Tirmidhi)

> The Prophet (peace be upon him) was asked: "Which deed is the dearest to Allah?" He replied: "To perform the daily prayers on time." (Bukhari)

The Prophet (peace be upon him) said: "The difference between us and them [the disbelievers] is that of Salah; so whoever abandons Salah certainly commits Kufr [disbelief]." (Tirmidhi)

These instructions from Allah and His Prophet (peace be upon him) make it very clear that the five daily prayers are a fundamental part of Islam. But for us to develop a true desire in our hearts to stand before our Creator in the prayer requires an understanding of the history of Salah.

Islam – the universal religion from the beginning of time

It is a common misconception that Islam began with the Prophet Muhammad (peace be upon him). In actual fact Islam ('submission to the will of Allah') is the true religion of all Prophets, from the Prophet Adam to the Prophet Muhammad (peace be upon them all). As human society developed over time so did their relationship with Allah, until revelation of the perfected religion to the final Messenger, the 'Seal of the Prophets' (peace be upon him):

Today, I have completed your religion for you; I gave My favour in full, and I am pleased that Islam is your religion. (Qur'an 5:3)

Humans have always prostrated before their Lord

From the Prophet Adam, every Prophet (peace be upon them all) was given forms of worship which involved Sujud (prostration); examples of which can still be found in the Torah and Gospel. But what about our five daily prayers?

The most difficult time in the Prophet's life

A few years prior to the migration of the Muslims from Makkah to Madinah, when the persecution they were experiencing from the Quraysh was reaching unbearable levels, the Prophet (peace be upon him) faced two personal tragedies. His first wife, Syedatuna Khadija (may Allah be pleased with her) passed away. She was the first person to accept Islam, the mother of his children, and an immense source of strength for him. Within the same year, his beloved uncle Abu Talib also passed away. His uncle had helped raise him and loved him more than his own children, and through him the Prophet had protection in the community.

Having limited success in calling the Arabs of Makkah to Islam the Prophet travelled to the neighbouring city of Taif. However, the elders rudely refused to talk to him and as he left, instructed their slaves and children to shout insults and pelt him with stones. The assault was so brutal that by the time the Prophet found refuge in a nearby orchard his shoes were filled with blood. This was a year of great sorrow and difficulty for the Prophet (peace be upon him).

Allah wants to remind His Prophet of his true station

Against this backdrop, one night the Prophet (peace be upon him) was asleep when the Archangel Jibra'il (may Allah be pleased with him) arrived to wake him. He was seated on the Buraq, a steed from Heaven which travels so fast it can plant its next step at the farthest point the eye can see. From Makkah they travelled to al-Aqsa Mosque in Jerusalem (al-Isra – 'the night journey'). Here the Prophet Muhammad led all of the Prophets of Allah, from the Prophet Adam to the Prophet Isa (peace be upon them all) as their Imam in some form of prayer.

Following this Syedina Jibra'il (may Allah be pleased with him) and the Prophet (peace be upon him) ascended to the Heavens (al-Mi'raj – literally translated as 'ladder', or ascension).

> **Glory to Him Who took His noble servant on a night journey from the Sacred Mosque to the farthest Mosque - whose surroundings we made holy - to show him Our signs. He is the Hearer, the Seeing. (Qur'an 17:1)**

As they went from the first to the seventh Heaven they again met with several Prophets and were shown many wondrous sights including the delights of Paradise and horrors of Hell. On the seventh Heaven they saw the Ka'bah of the Angels (al-Baitul Ma'mur – 'the oft visited house').

From here Syedina Jibra'il (may Allah be pleased with him) took him to Sidrat'al-Muntaha – a huge lote tree, which is his station from where he awaits Allah's command. Here, the Archangel told the Prophet (peace be upon him) that he would have to continue alone, if the Archangel was to take another step, his wings would be burnt.

The Prophet was brought into the Divine presence

Allah brought the Prophet (peace be upon him) into His presence, and unveiled Himself to the Prophet, as described in Surah Najm:

> ...Then they drew near, very near. The distance between two bows held together. So he revealed to His servant what he revealed. His heart didn't deny what he saw. (Qur'an 53:8-11)

And a few verses later:

> ...his eyes didn't wander nor turn to the side as he witnessed the greatest signs of His Lord. (Qur'an 53:17-18)

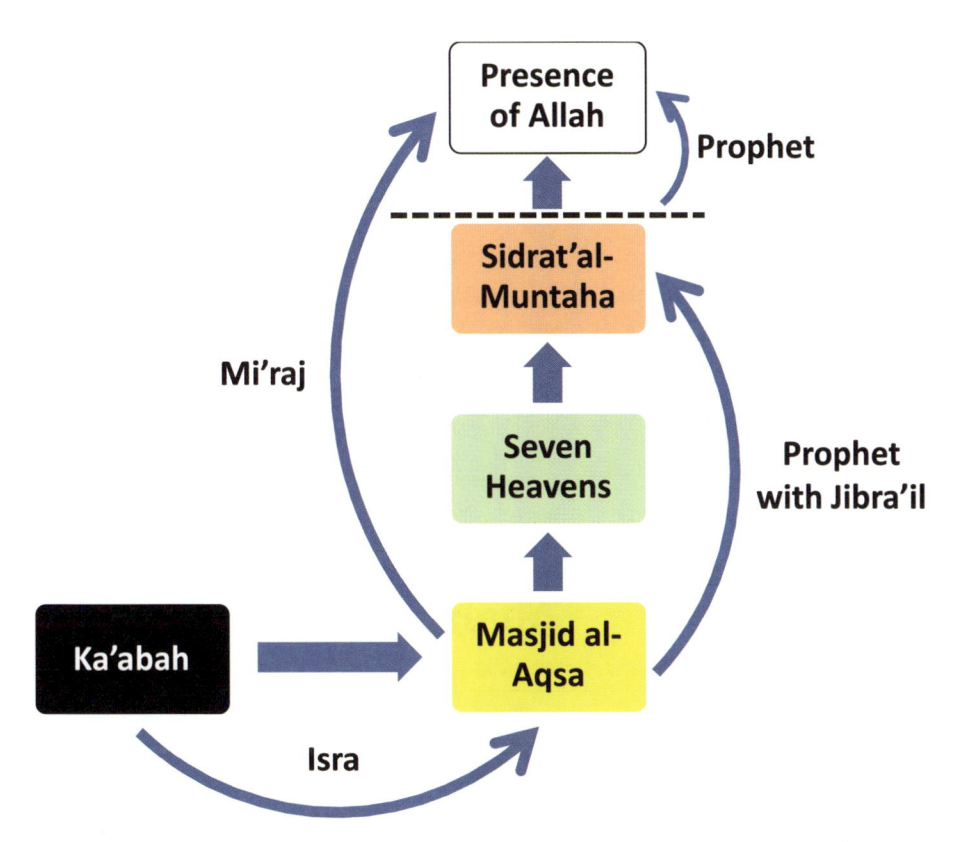

Diagram:
- Ka'abah → Masjid al-Aqsa (Isra) — Prophet (riding on Buraq), with Jibra'il
- Masjid al-Aqsa → Seven Heavens → Sidrat'al-Muntaha — Prophet with Jibra'il
- Sidrat'al-Muntaha → Presence of Allah (Mi'raj) — Prophet

The Prophet's love for us, and Allah's gift for us

Consider this meeting between Allah and His beloved; not a dream but the Prophet (peace be upon him) has travelled in mind, body and soul, to a station that is unique for him alone. Perhaps it is no coincidence that this miraculous journey occurred at the time of such sadness and difficulty, a reminder from Allah that this is his true station.

And look at the mercy and compassion of the Prophet (peace be upon him). During such a meeting he is still remembering his Ummah (community of followers – from his lifetime to the Day of Judgement), begging for our forgiveness. During this most exalted of meetings Allah gave His beloved a gift for us: the prayer (Salah).

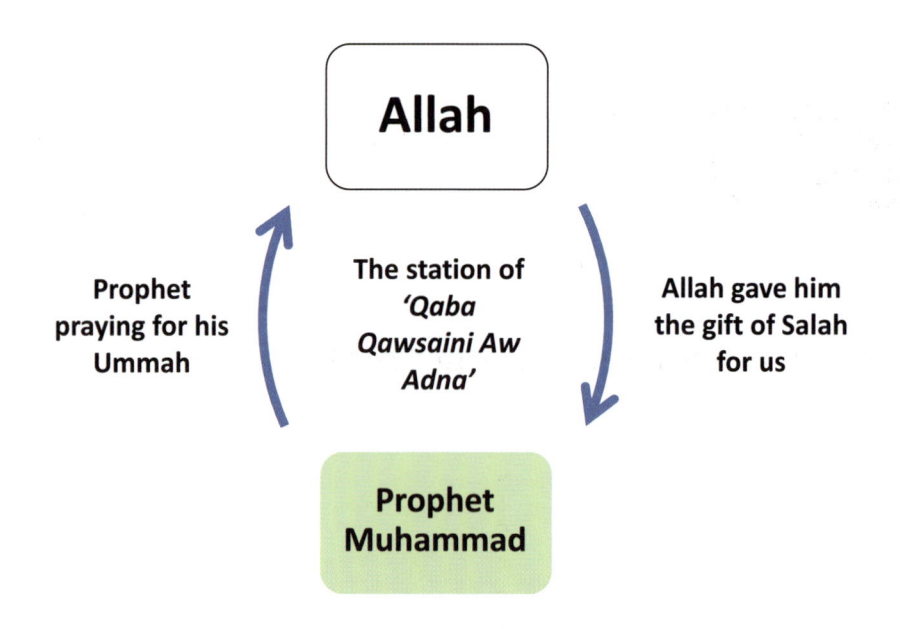

Allah

The station of 'Qaba Qawsaini Aw Adna'

Prophet praying for his Ummah

Allah gave him the gift of Salah for us

Prophet Muhammad

Virtue of Salah

The immense blessings of Salah are mentioned in the Qur'an and Hadith:

> *...and regularly perform their prayers. Such people are the true heirs, they will inherit Paradise, living in it forever. (Qur'an 23:9-11)*

> *...Recite the Book revealed to you, messenger, and perform the prayer. Without doubt, prayer protects from indecency and evil; and to remember Allah is greater still; and Allah knows well what you do. (Qur'an 29:45)*

> *The Prophet (peace be upon him) said, "If there was a river at your door and you took a bath in it five times a day, would you notice any dirt?" They (his companions) replied, "Not a trace of dirt would be left." He said, "That is the example of the five daily prayers by which Allah removes sins." (Bukhari)*

Worshipping Allah with mind, body and soul

Salah is a unique form of physical and spiritual worship in which specific recitations are linked to actions or postures. For example, the Sujud is a particularly favourite worship in the eyes of Allah.

We recite Subhana rabbiyal a'alaa (glory be to my Lord, The Most High) while lowering the highest part of our body (our forehead) to the ground; an action which is impermissible (Haram) to carry out in front of anyone or anything else. The Prophet (peace be upon him) told us:

> **The nearest a servant comes to his Lord is when he is prostrating himself, so make supplication in this state. (Muslim)**

In each unit (Rak'ah) of Salah we recite Surah Al-Fatihah. Regarding these seven 'oft repeated' verses (the Surah is also known as 'the mother of the Qur'an'), Allah says:

> *"I have divided Al-Fatihah into two halves between Myself and My servant:*
> - *When My servant says, 'Praise be to Allah, the Lord of all the worlds,' Allah says, `My servant has praised Me.'*
> - *When My servant says, 'the All-Merciful, the Most Merciful,' Allah says, `My servant has glorified Me.'*
> - *When he says, 'the King of the Day of Judgement,' Allah says, `My servant has related all matters to Me.'*
> - *When he says, 'You alone we worship. You alone we ask for help,' Allah says, `This is between Me and My servant, and My servant shall acquire what he seeks.'*

- *When he says, 'Guide us on the Straight Path, the Path of those You have blessed, not of those with anger on them, nor of the misguided,' Allah says, `This is for My servant, and My servant shall have what he asked for.'" (Muslim)*

Conversing with Allah – going on our own Mi'raj

These examples show us that during Salah we are engaged in a very real conversation with Allah. He is listening to our every word and indeed replying to our supplications.

The Prophet (peace be upon him) told us, "the Salah is the Mi'raj of the Mu'min [believer who submits completely to the will of Allah]", but this is not applicable to just any Salah. This is a prayer where our attention is towards Allah alone and we have left the world behind. This is a prayer where, as the Prophet told us regarding Ihsan (excellence): "you are praying as if you are seeing Allah, and if you cannot do that, then with the surety that Allah is seeing you." Then we will be in the presence of Allah, on our own Mi'raj.

How will we know when we have achieved this? Because we will feel overwhelmed, our heart will tremble with awe of Allah, tears will stream from our eyes, and we will wish the prayer would never end. When we have finished, our heart will feel at peace but we will long for the next prayer, so we can once again stand in front of our Creator and go on our Mi'raj, into His presence.

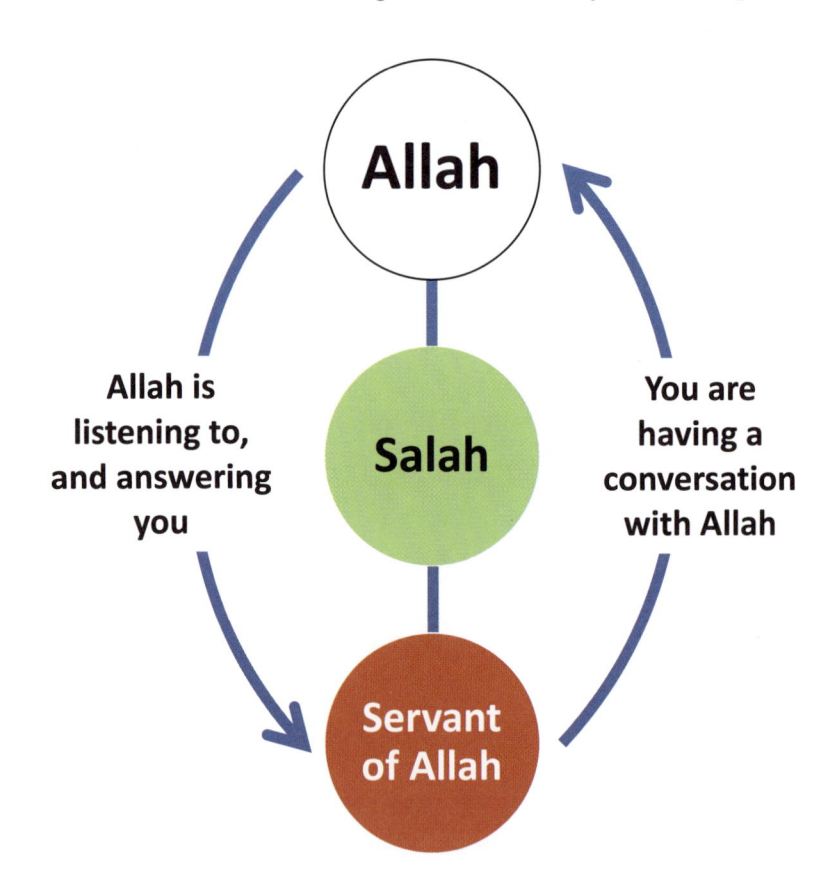

```
         Allah
    ↙            ↖
Allah is          You are
listening to,    having a
and answering    conversation
you              with Allah
    ↘            ↗
      Servant
      of Allah
```

(Center: Salah)

How to increase Khushu during Salah

The believers have succeeded: those who are humbly focused in their prayer (Qur'an 23:1-2)

The purpose of this chapter is to provide a practical guide to achieve this level of Khushu (concentration and humility). However, we must remember the immeasurable blessing of Allah that He has given us Hidayah (guidance) to pray Salah even if we lack concentration. Knowing that our prayer is deficient and having the desire to improve it is a further blessing from Him. We should pray to Allah for help with this struggle, remembering the Hadith Qudsi:

> *"He who draws close to Me a hand's span, I will draw close to him an arm's length. And whoever draws near Me an arm's length, I will draw near him a fathom's length. And whoever comes to Me walking, I will go to him running..." (Bukhari)*

1) Praying in the Mosque with Jama'ah

We should go to the Mosque to perform our prayer with congregation. This means leaving our normal environment in which we are surrounded by people engrossed in worldly affairs and our worldly possessions. So not only is there the physical act of distancing ourselves from the world but also the psychological act when we make the intention, prepare for, and then leave our house to go to the house of Allah, to pray before Him. Being surrounded by others who are there for the same purpose protects us from distraction and helps with concentration.

If we are praying at home, or in the case of women (according to the Hanafi school of religious law), then we should have an allocated prayer room where there is no noise or distractions and within it we just have the things needed to perform the prayer, recite Qur'an and other Dhikr'Allah. It is also most beneficial if the whole family can pray at the same time.

> *The Prophet (peace be upon him) said: "Prayer in congregation is superior to prayer alone by twenty-seven degrees." (Bukhari).*
>
> *The Prophet (peace be upon him) said, "Whoever prays Isha in congregation, it is as if he spent half the night in prayer, and whoever prays Isha and Fajr in congregation, it is as if he spent the whole night in prayer." (Abu Dawood)*

2) Performing the Wudu with intention

When we make Wudu it should be with the intention that we are purifying ourselves with the purpose of standing before Allah. In this way our concentration for the prayer begins from the ablution. The ablution should ideally be redone before every prayer. This also means avoiding doing anything else in between the ablution and standing for the prayer.

The Prophet (peace be upon him) said: "...the key to Salah is Wudu." (Tirmidhi)

3) Clarifying our intention for Salah

We should take a few minutes to sit before starting Salah. If going to the Mosque to pray in congregation, we should arrive a few minutes early so we do not have to rush to join in. If we are praying at home we should not delay the Salah until its time is about to run out. The purpose is to contemplate what we are about to do.

What are we doing when we perform the Prayer? We stand before Allah, we talk to Him, He listens to and sees us, and He responds to our words. This is why the Prophet (peace be upon him) described the prayer as a Mi'raj; just as he entered the presence of, and spoke with Allah on the night of the ascension, we are doing something similar when performing Salah.

By taking a few minutes before we start to think about this, it will help improve our concentration during the prayer. Furthermore, before we start, we should recite a few Quranic verses to protect us from the whisperings of the devil:

The Ta'awwudh (A`udhu billah)

> *I seek refuge in Allah from Shaitan, the accursed one*

The Tasmiyah (Bismillah)

In the name of Allah, the Kind, the Caring

Surah Al-Nas:

Say: "I seek refuge in the Lord of the people, the King of the people, the God of the people, from the evil of the sneaking whisperer, who whispers into people›s hearts and minds, from among the jinn or the people. (Qur'an 114)

4) Controlling our thoughts during Salah

We should reflect upon what we are thinking about during the prayer itself. Our everyday thoughts are often related to work, family or money. Sometimes we perform the actions and recitations of Salah on autopilot while our concentration on these worldly matters becomes magnified, they are all we can think about. This results in forgetting how many Rak'ah we have prayed and sometimes we complete the Salah and it feels as if we have not even prayed.

How shameful is this situation? If we pray like this, if all we are thinking about is worldly matters then what are we achieving by praying? We are merely fulfilling a ritual with very little benefit to ourselves. But also consider, when we perform Salah we are standing before the King of kings, The Creator and Sustainer of the Universe. These problems and worries we have, these worldly matters which preoccupy us, it is Allah who is ultimately responsible for them, He is the One who has absolute control over all things.

> *...They claim Allah has adopted a son. Glory be to Him! The Heavens and the Earth belong to Him; everything obeys Him, The Creator of The Heavens and the Earth. When He decides on any matter, He only says: "Be!" And there it is. (Qur'an 2:116-117)*

> *The Prophet (peace be upon him) said, "When you ask, ask Allah. When you seek aid and succour, seek it from Allah. And know, that if the entire nation got together to benefit you in some way, they could never benefit you at all except for that which Allah had already decreed for you. And, if they all got together to harm you in some way, they could do you no harm except for that which Allah had already decreed for you." (Tirmidhi)*

So if Allah wills, even if we believe every avenue has been explored and our situation is hopeless, everything will work itself out for the best, beyond all expectation. Similarly, no matter how happy and stress-free we currently are, if He wills our world could be turned upside down from one second to the next, with no pre-warning. So when standing before Allah, praying to Him, speaking with Him, asking Him for His help, what need do we have to worry about anything?

Therefore, while performing Salah we should remember who we are standing before, who we are talking with, who is listening to our recitations, and in doing so we should feel a sense of peace and calm and be able to free ourselves from the worries of this world.

> ...those who believe, their hearts will find peace in Allah's remembrance." The fact is, hearts find peace in the remembrance of Allah! (Qur'an 13:28)

5) Considering our words and actions

As we pray we should actively think about what we are reciting and doing. Arabic verses should be recited slowly and movements performed calmly. When standing before someone important, we would speak carefully, we would not be in a rush, mixing our words so they do not make sense, nor would we be in a hurry to leave. If someone came to ask us for help, in such a rush that we could not understand what they were saying, would we help them?

Salah should not be made in silence. The Prophet (peace be upon him) taught us that the words should be just loud enough for us to hear them. When we hear ourselves say the words it will focus our attention. The meanings of the Arabic verses that are recited should be learnt in order to understand how different verses relate to different movements and how we really are having a conversation with Allah.

The most often repeated phrase within Salah is 'Allahu Akbar', which we hear recited within the Adhan, to start the Salah, and whenever changing position within the Salah. This can be translated as 'there is nothing greater than Allah'. By concentrating on the meaning of this phrase we are repeatedly reminding ourselves during the Salah that whatever else we might be getting distracted with, it is insignificant compared to Allah.

So in summary, while performing Salah we should remember that we are standing before the King of kings, the Lord of the universe; we should perform our actions in a calm manner, recite the Arabic verses slowly, loud enough so we can hear them and with understanding of their meaning.

6) Performing the full Salah

Many Muslims just pray the Fard (obligatory part of the Prayer) missing out the Sunnah and Nawafil (supererogatory parts). If Salah is being performed purely because it is a ritual and has to be done, then performing the minimum and leaving the rest would make sense. But if it is performed with the wish to stand before Allah and speak with Him five times a day, to obtain the feeling of calm and peace only found within the remembrance of Allah, then we would want it to last as long as possible. In which case, it makes no sense to perform the Fard and leave the Sunnah and Nawafil. As per the Hadith Qudsi:

> "My slave does not draw closer to Me by anything more beloved to Me than that which I have made obligatory upon him, and My slave continues to draw closer to Me by doing Nawafil (supererogatory) deeds until I love him, and if I love him I will be his hearing with which he hears, his vision with which he sees, his hand with which he strikes and his foot with which he walks. If he were to ask of Me, I would surely give to him; if he were to seek refuge with Me, I would surely grant him refuge." (Bukhari)

The supererogatory parts of Salah can also make up for deficiencies in the obligatory parts:

> The Prophet (peace be upon him) said, "...if there is something defective in his obligatory prayers, then the Almighty Lord will say: "See if my servant has any voluntary prayers that can complete what is insufficient in his obligatory prayers."" (Tirmidhi)

7)   Making time for Dua and Dhikr'Allah after the Salah

Dua and Dhikr'Allah should be made after completion of Salah. We should raise our hands and thank Allah from the bottom of our heart for His countless blessings, including the ability and inclination to perform Salah. We should ask Him to grant us Khushu during Salah. Following this, we should sit, if even for a few minutes, in silence, eyes closed, attention turned inwards towards our heart, remembering Allah.

In the same way that concentrating during the prayer is difficult, so too is concentrating during Dhikr'Allah. The two work in harmony; meditation helps with gaining concentration during Salah, and Salah helps with gaining concentrating during meditation.

> *If My servants ask you about Me, tell them that I am near, I answer the prayer of the prayerful whenever he prays to Me. So, let them obey Me, and believe in Me so they may be guided. (Qur'an 2:186)*
>
> *'There is no Muslim who calls upon his Lord with a Dua in which there is no sin, or severing of family ties, but Allah will give him one of three things:*
> - *Either He will answer his prayer quickly, or*
> - *He will store (the reward for) it in the Hereafter, or*
> - *He will divert an equivalent evil away from him.' [Tirmidhi]*
>
> *So, remember Me, and I shall remember you. (Qur'an 2:152)*
>
> *"...who remember Allah standing, sitting and lying down, and think about the creation of the Heavens and the Earth, prayerfully saying, "Our Lord, You haven't created this in vain, Glory be to You! Save us from the punishment of the Fire. (Qur'an 3:191)*

The Prophet (peace be upon him) said, "Whenever people sit to remember Allah, Angels cover them (spreading their wings over them) and divine mercy envelops them; inner peace descends on them and Allah mentions them to those who are with Him." (Muslim)

Summary

I have outlined seven points to improve Khushu during Salah:

- Going to the Mosque to pray in Jama'ah, or if at home, in a separate prayer room free from worldly distractions and noise. In this way we physically enact the spiritual action of leaving the world to enter the presence of Allah.

- Performing Wudu before every prayer with the intention of purifying ourselves for standing before Allah, and not getting distracted between performing the ablution and the prayer.

- Taking a few minutes before starting Salah to sit and prepare ourselves by considering what we are about to do, Who we are about to stand in front of, and recite the Ta'awwudh, the Tasmiyah, and Surah Al-Nas.

- Leaving all worldly thoughts and worries behind during Salah, to truly be in the presence of the Almighty, the Creator, the One who has control over all things, and so to be at peace.

- This will manifest itself as calmly performing the movements and reciting the Arabic verses, just loud enough so we can hear ourselves and with understanding.
- If we have achieved this then we will complete Salah with the Sunnah and Nawafil and will not be in a rush to finish.
- Once we have finished, raising our hands, expressing gratitude (Shukr), asking Allah for whatever our heart desires including help in obtaining Khushu in Salah, and then sitting for a few minutes, closing our eyes, focussing on our heart, and engaging in meditation in Dhikr'Allah.

On the following pages I have included tables to record the number of prayers we perform each day, whether we perform them with congregation (or at home for women), and what degree of concentration and humility we had during the prayer. In this way, it will become apparent to us if we are consistently missing a certain prayer (e.g. Fajr or Isha), it will encourage us to pray in the Mosque (for men), or a quiet room at home (for women), and it will force us to assess if over time we are increasing our level of concentration and humility.

When we practice anything in life (e.g. work, cooking, sport, a musical instrument) our aim is to improve, to get better at it each time we do it. Salah should be no different. We should make an intention that each time we pray it will be a little bit better than the last time. If we could do this imagine how beautiful our prayers would become within a day, a week, a month, a year, or a lifetime?

Salah	Prayed?	In Jama'ah / in quiet room at home?	Level of Khushu (%)
Fajr	Yes / No	Yes / No	100 / 75 / 50 / 25 / 0
Dhuhr	Yes / No	Yes / No	100 / 75 / 50 / 25 / 0
Asr	Yes / No	Yes / No	100 / 75 / 50 / 25 / 0
Maghrib	Yes / No	Yes / No	100 / 75 / 50 / 25 / 0
Isha	Yes / No	Yes / No	100 / 75 / 50 / 25 / 0

Date: ___/___/___

Fajr	Yes / No	Yes / No	100 / 75 / 50 / 25 / 0
Dhuhr	Yes / No	Yes / No	100 / 75 / 50 / 25 / 0
Asr	Yes / No	Yes / No	100 / 75 / 50 / 25 / 0
Maghrib	Yes / No	Yes / No	100 / 75 / 50 / 25 / 0
Isha	Yes / No	Yes / No	100 / 75 / 50 / 25 / 0

Date: ___/___/___

Fajr	Yes / No	Yes / No	100 / 75 / 50 / 25 / 0
Dhuhr	Yes / No	Yes / No	100 / 75 / 50 / 25 / 0
Asr	Yes / No	Yes / No	100 / 75 / 50 / 25 / 0
Maghrib	Yes / No	Yes / No	100 / 75 / 50 / 25 / 0
Isha	Yes / No	Yes / No	100 / 75 / 50 / 25 / 0

The Salah: Praying with Khushu

Salah	Prayed?	In Jama'ah / in quiet room at home?	Level of Khushu (%)

Date: ___/___/___

Salah	Prayed?	In Jama'ah / in quiet room at home?	Level of Khushu (%)
Fajr	Yes / No	Yes / No	100 / 75 / 50 / 25 / 0
Dhuhr	Yes / No	Yes / No	100 / 75 / 50 / 25 / 0
Asr	Yes / No	Yes / No	100 / 75 / 50 / 25 / 0
Maghrib	Yes / No	Yes / No	100 / 75 / 50 / 25 / 0
Isha	Yes / No	Yes / No	100 / 75 / 50 / 25 / 0

Date: ___/___/___

Salah	Prayed?	In Jama'ah / in quiet room at home?	Level of Khushu (%)
Fajr	Yes / No	Yes / No	100 / 75 / 50 / 25 / 0
Dhuhr	Yes / No	Yes / No	100 / 75 / 50 / 25 / 0
Asr	Yes / No	Yes / No	100 / 75 / 50 / 25 / 0
Maghrib	Yes / No	Yes / No	100 / 75 / 50 / 25 / 0
Isha	Yes / No	Yes / No	100 / 75 / 50 / 25 / 0

Drawing closer to Allah and His Prophet A Practical Guide

Salah	Prayed?	In Jama'ah / in quiet room at home?	Level of Khushu (%)

Date: ___/___/___

Salah	Prayed?	In Jama'ah / in quiet room at home?	Level of Khushu (%)
Fajr	Yes / No	Yes / No	100 / 75 / 50 / 25 / 0
Dhuhr	Yes / No	Yes / No	100 / 75 / 50 / 25 / 0
Asr	Yes / No	Yes / No	100 / 75 / 50 / 25 / 0
Maghrib	Yes / No	Yes / No	100 / 75 / 50 / 25 / 0
Isha	Yes / No	Yes / No	100 / 75 / 50 / 25 / 0

Date: ___/___/___

Salah	Prayed?	In Jama'ah / in quiet room at home?	Level of Khushu (%)
Fajr	Yes / No	Yes / No	100 / 75 / 50 / 25 / 0
Dhuhr	Yes / No	Yes / No	100 / 75 / 50 / 25 / 0
Asr	Yes / No	Yes / No	100 / 75 / 50 / 25 / 0
Maghrib	Yes / No	Yes / No	100 / 75 / 50 / 25 / 0
Isha	Yes / No	Yes / No	100 / 75 / 50 / 25 / 0

The Salah: Praying with Khushu

Salah	Prayed?	In Jama'ah / in quiet room at home?	Level of Khushu (%)

Date: ___/___/___

Salah	Prayed?	In Jama'ah / in quiet room at home?	Level of Khushu (%)
Fajr	Yes / No	Yes / No	100 / 75 / 50 / 25 / 0
Dhuhr	Yes / No	Yes / No	100 / 75 / 50 / 25 / 0
Asr	Yes / No	Yes / No	100 / 75 / 50 / 25 / 0
Maghrib	Yes / No	Yes / No	100 / 75 / 50 / 25 / 0
Isha	Yes / No	Yes / No	100 / 75 / 50 / 25 / 0

Date: ___/___/___

Salah	Prayed?	In Jama'ah / in quiet room at home?	Level of Khushu (%)
Fajr	Yes / No	Yes / No	100 / 75 / 50 / 25 / 0
Dhuhr	Yes / No	Yes / No	100 / 75 / 50 / 25 / 0
Asr	Yes / No	Yes / No	100 / 75 / 50 / 25 / 0
Maghrib	Yes / No	Yes / No	100 / 75 / 50 / 25 / 0
Isha	Yes / No	Yes / No	100 / 75 / 50 / 25 / 0

Drawing closer to Allah and His Prophet A Practical Guide

Salah	Prayed?	In Jama'ah / in quiet room at home?	Level of Khushu (%)

Date: ___/___/___

Salah	Prayed?	In Jama'ah / in quiet room at home?	Level of Khushu (%)
Fajr	Yes / No	Yes / No	100 / 75 / 50 / 25 / 0
Dhuhr	Yes / No	Yes / No	100 / 75 / 50 / 25 / 0
Asr	Yes / No	Yes / No	100 / 75 / 50 / 25 / 0
Maghrib	Yes / No	Yes / No	100 / 75 / 50 / 25 / 0
Isha	Yes / No	Yes / No	100 / 75 / 50 / 25 / 0

Date: ___/___/___

Salah	Prayed?	In Jama'ah / in quiet room at home?	Level of Khushu (%)
Fajr	Yes / No	Yes / No	100 / 75 / 50 / 25 / 0
Dhuhr	Yes / No	Yes / No	100 / 75 / 50 / 25 / 0
Asr	Yes / No	Yes / No	100 / 75 / 50 / 25 / 0
Maghrib	Yes / No	Yes / No	100 / 75 / 50 / 25 / 0
Isha	Yes / No	Yes / No	100 / 75 / 50 / 25 / 0

The Salah: Praying with Khushu

Salah	Prayed?	In Jama'ah / in quiet room at home?	Level of Khushu (%)

Date: ___/___/___

Salah	Prayed?	In Jama'ah / in quiet room at home?	Level of Khushu (%)
Fajr	Yes / No	Yes / No	100 / 75 / 50 / 25 / 0
Dhuhr	Yes / No	Yes / No	100 / 75 / 50 / 25 / 0
Asr	Yes / No	Yes / No	100 / 75 / 50 / 25 / 0
Maghrib	Yes / No	Yes / No	100 / 75 / 50 / 25 / 0
Isha	Yes / No	Yes / No	100 / 75 / 50 / 25 / 0

Date: ___/___/___

Salah	Prayed?	In Jama'ah / in quiet room at home?	Level of Khushu (%)
Fajr	Yes / No	Yes / No	100 / 75 / 50 / 25 / 0
Dhuhr	Yes / No	Yes / No	100 / 75 / 50 / 25 / 0
Asr	Yes / No	Yes / No	100 / 75 / 50 / 25 / 0
Maghrib	Yes / No	Yes / No	100 / 75 / 50 / 25 / 0
Isha	Yes / No	Yes / No	100 / 75 / 50 / 25 / 0

Salah	Prayed?	In Jama'ah / in quiet room at home?	Level of Khushu (%)
Fajr	Yes / No	Yes / No	100 / 75 / 50 / 25 / 0

Date: ___/___/___

Salah	Prayed?	In Jama'ah / in quiet room at home?	Level of Khushu (%)
Fajr	Yes / No	Yes / No	100 / 75 / 50 / 25 / 0
Dhuhr	Yes / No	Yes / No	100 / 75 / 50 / 25 / 0
Asr	Yes / No	Yes / No	100 / 75 / 50 / 25 / 0
Maghrib	Yes / No	Yes / No	100 / 75 / 50 / 25 / 0
Isha	Yes / No	Yes / No	100 / 75 / 50 / 25 / 0

Date: ___/___/___

Salah	Prayed?	In Jama'ah / in quiet room at home?	Level of Khushu (%)
Fajr	Yes / No	Yes / No	100 / 75 / 50 / 25 / 0
Dhuhr	Yes / No	Yes / No	100 / 75 / 50 / 25 / 0
Asr	Yes / No	Yes / No	100 / 75 / 50 / 25 / 0
Maghrib	Yes / No	Yes / No	100 / 75 / 50 / 25 / 0
Isha	Yes / No	Yes / No	100 / 75 / 50 / 25 / 0

The Salah: Praying with Khushu

Salah	Prayed?	In Jama'ah / in quiet room at home?	Level of Khushu (%)

Date: ___/___/___

Salah	Prayed?	In Jama'ah / in quiet room at home?	Level of Khushu (%)
Fajr	Yes / No	Yes / No	100 / 75 / 50 / 25 / 0
Dhuhr	Yes / No	Yes / No	100 / 75 / 50 / 25 / 0
Asr	Yes / No	Yes / No	100 / 75 / 50 / 25 / 0
Maghrib	Yes / No	Yes / No	100 / 75 / 50 / 25 / 0
Isha	Yes / No	Yes / No	100 / 75 / 50 / 25 / 0

Date: ___/___/___

Salah	Prayed?	In Jama'ah / in quiet room at home?	Level of Khushu (%)
Fajr	Yes / No	Yes / No	100 / 75 / 50 / 25 / 0
Dhuhr	Yes / No	Yes / No	100 / 75 / 50 / 25 / 0
Asr	Yes / No	Yes / No	100 / 75 / 50 / 25 / 0
Maghrib	Yes / No	Yes / No	100 / 75 / 50 / 25 / 0
Isha	Yes / No	Yes / No	100 / 75 / 50 / 25 / 0

Salah	Prayed?	In Jama'ah / in quiet room at home?	Level of Khushu (%)
Fajr	Yes / No	Yes / No	100 / 75 / 50 / 25 / 0
Dhuhr	Yes / No	Yes / No	100 / 75 / 50 / 25 / 0
Asr	Yes / No	Yes / No	100 / 75 / 50 / 25 / 0
Maghrib	Yes / No	Yes / No	100 / 75 / 50 / 25 / 0
Isha	Yes / No	Yes / No	100 / 75 / 50 / 25 / 0

Date: ___/___/___

Salah	Prayed?	In Jama'ah / in quiet room at home?	Level of Khushu (%)
Fajr	Yes / No	Yes / No	100 / 75 / 50 / 25 / 0
Dhuhr	Yes / No	Yes / No	100 / 75 / 50 / 25 / 0
Asr	Yes / No	Yes / No	100 / 75 / 50 / 25 / 0
Maghrib	Yes / No	Yes / No	100 / 75 / 50 / 25 / 0
Isha	Yes / No	Yes / No	100 / 75 / 50 / 25 / 0

Date: ___/___/___

The Salah: Praying with Khushu

Salah	Prayed?	In Jama'ah / in quiet room at home?	Level of Khushu (%)

Date: ___/___/___

Salah	Prayed?	In Jama'ah / in quiet room at home?	Level of Khushu (%)
Fajr	Yes / No	Yes / No	100 / 75 / 50 / 25 / 0
Dhuhr	Yes / No	Yes / No	100 / 75 / 50 / 25 / 0
Asr	Yes / No	Yes / No	100 / 75 / 50 / 25 / 0
Maghrib	Yes / No	Yes / No	100 / 75 / 50 / 25 / 0
Isha	Yes / No	Yes / No	100 / 75 / 50 / 25 / 0

Date: ___/___/___

Salah	Prayed?	In Jama'ah / in quiet room at home?	Level of Khushu (%)
Fajr	Yes / No	Yes / No	100 / 75 / 50 / 25 / 0
Dhuhr	Yes / No	Yes / No	100 / 75 / 50 / 25 / 0
Asr	Yes / No	Yes / No	100 / 75 / 50 / 25 / 0
Maghrib	Yes / No	Yes / No	100 / 75 / 50 / 25 / 0
Isha	Yes / No	Yes / No	100 / 75 / 50 / 25 / 0

Salah	Prayed?	In Jama'ah / in quiet room at home?	Level of Khushu (%)
Fajr	Yes / No	Yes / No	100 / 75 / 50 / 25 / 0
Dhuhr	Yes / No	Yes / No	100 / 75 / 50 / 25 / 0
Asr	Yes / No	Yes / No	100 / 75 / 50 / 25 / 0
Maghrib	Yes / No	Yes / No	100 / 75 / 50 / 25 / 0
Isha	Yes / No	Yes / No	100 / 75 / 50 / 25 / 0

Date: ___/___/___

Fajr	Yes / No	Yes / No	100 / 75 / 50 / 25 / 0
Dhuhr	Yes / No	Yes / No	100 / 75 / 50 / 25 / 0
Asr	Yes / No	Yes / No	100 / 75 / 50 / 25 / 0
Maghrib	Yes / No	Yes / No	100 / 75 / 50 / 25 / 0
Isha	Yes / No	Yes / No	100 / 75 / 50 / 25 / 0

Date: ___/___/___

Fajr	Yes / No	Yes / No	100 / 75 / 50 / 25 / 0
Dhuhr	Yes / No	Yes / No	100 / 75 / 50 / 25 / 0
Asr	Yes / No	Yes / No	100 / 75 / 50 / 25 / 0
Maghrib	Yes / No	Yes / No	100 / 75 / 50 / 25 / 0
Isha	Yes / No	Yes / No	100 / 75 / 50 / 25 / 0

The Salah: Praying with Khushu

Salah	Prayed?	In Jama'ah / in quiet room at home?	Level of Khushu (%)

Date: ___/___/___

Salah	Prayed?	In Jama'ah / in quiet room at home?	Level of Khushu (%)
Fajr	Yes / No	Yes / No	100 / 75 / 50 / 25 / 0
Dhuhr	Yes / No	Yes / No	100 / 75 / 50 / 25 / 0
Asr	Yes / No	Yes / No	100 / 75 / 50 / 25 / 0
Maghrib	Yes / No	Yes / No	100 / 75 / 50 / 25 / 0
Isha	Yes / No	Yes / No	100 / 75 / 50 / 25 / 0

Date: ___/___/___

Salah	Prayed?	In Jama'ah / in quiet room at home?	Level of Khushu (%)
Fajr	Yes / No	Yes / No	100 / 75 / 50 / 25 / 0
Dhuhr	Yes / No	Yes / No	100 / 75 / 50 / 25 / 0
Asr	Yes / No	Yes / No	100 / 75 / 50 / 25 / 0
Maghrib	Yes / No	Yes / No	100 / 75 / 50 / 25 / 0
Isha	Yes / No	Yes / No	100 / 75 / 50 / 25 / 0

Drawing closer to Allah and His Prophet A Practical Guide

Salah	Prayed?	In Jama'ah / in quiet room at home?	Level of Khushu (%)

Date: ___/___/___

Salah	Prayed?	In Jama'ah / in quiet room at home?	Level of Khushu (%)
Fajr	Yes / No	Yes / No	100 / 75 / 50 / 25 / 0
Dhuhr	Yes / No	Yes / No	100 / 75 / 50 / 25 / 0
Asr	Yes / No	Yes / No	100 / 75 / 50 / 25 / 0
Maghrib	Yes / No	Yes / No	100 / 75 / 50 / 25 / 0
Isha	Yes / No	Yes / No	100 / 75 / 50 / 25 / 0

Date: ___/___/___

Salah	Prayed?	In Jama'ah / in quiet room at home?	Level of Khushu (%)
Fajr	Yes / No	Yes / No	100 / 75 / 50 / 25 / 0
Dhuhr	Yes / No	Yes / No	100 / 75 / 50 / 25 / 0
Asr	Yes / No	Yes / No	100 / 75 / 50 / 25 / 0
Maghrib	Yes / No	Yes / No	100 / 75 / 50 / 25 / 0
Isha	Yes / No	Yes / No	100 / 75 / 50 / 25 / 0

The Salah: Praying with Khushu

Salah	Prayed?	In Jama'ah / in quiet room at home?	Level of Khushu (%)

Date: ___/___/___

Salah	Prayed?	In Jama'ah / in quiet room at home?	Level of Khushu (%)
Fajr	Yes / No	Yes / No	100 / 75 / 50 / 25 / 0
Dhuhr	Yes / No	Yes / No	100 / 75 / 50 / 25 / 0
Asr	Yes / No	Yes / No	100 / 75 / 50 / 25 / 0
Maghrib	Yes / No	Yes / No	100 / 75 / 50 / 25 / 0
Isha	Yes / No	Yes / No	100 / 75 / 50 / 25 / 0

Date: ___/___/___

Salah	Prayed?	In Jama'ah / in quiet room at home?	Level of Khushu (%)
Fajr	Yes / No	Yes / No	100 / 75 / 50 / 25 / 0
Dhuhr	Yes / No	Yes / No	100 / 75 / 50 / 25 / 0
Asr	Yes / No	Yes / No	100 / 75 / 50 / 25 / 0
Maghrib	Yes / No	Yes / No	100 / 75 / 50 / 25 / 0
Isha	Yes / No	Yes / No	100 / 75 / 50 / 25 / 0

Salah	Prayed?	In Jama'ah / in quiet room at home?	Level of Khushu (%)
Fajr	Yes / No	Yes / No	100 / 75 / 50 / 25 / 0
Dhuhr	Yes / No	Yes / No	100 / 75 / 50 / 25 / 0
Asr	Yes / No	Yes / No	100 / 75 / 50 / 25 / 0
Maghrib	Yes / No	Yes / No	100 / 75 / 50 / 25 / 0
Isha	Yes / No	Yes / No	100 / 75 / 50 / 25 / 0

Date: ___/___/___

Fajr	Yes / No	Yes / No	100 / 75 / 50 / 25 / 0
Dhuhr	Yes / No	Yes / No	100 / 75 / 50 / 25 / 0
Asr	Yes / No	Yes / No	100 / 75 / 50 / 25 / 0
Maghrib	Yes / No	Yes / No	100 / 75 / 50 / 25 / 0
Isha	Yes / No	Yes / No	100 / 75 / 50 / 25 / 0

Date: ___/___/___

Fajr	Yes / No	Yes / No	100 / 75 / 50 / 25 / 0
Dhuhr	Yes / No	Yes / No	100 / 75 / 50 / 25 / 0
Asr	Yes / No	Yes / No	100 / 75 / 50 / 25 / 0
Maghrib	Yes / No	Yes / No	100 / 75 / 50 / 25 / 0
Isha	Yes / No	Yes / No	100 / 75 / 50 / 25 / 0

The Salah: Praying with Khushu

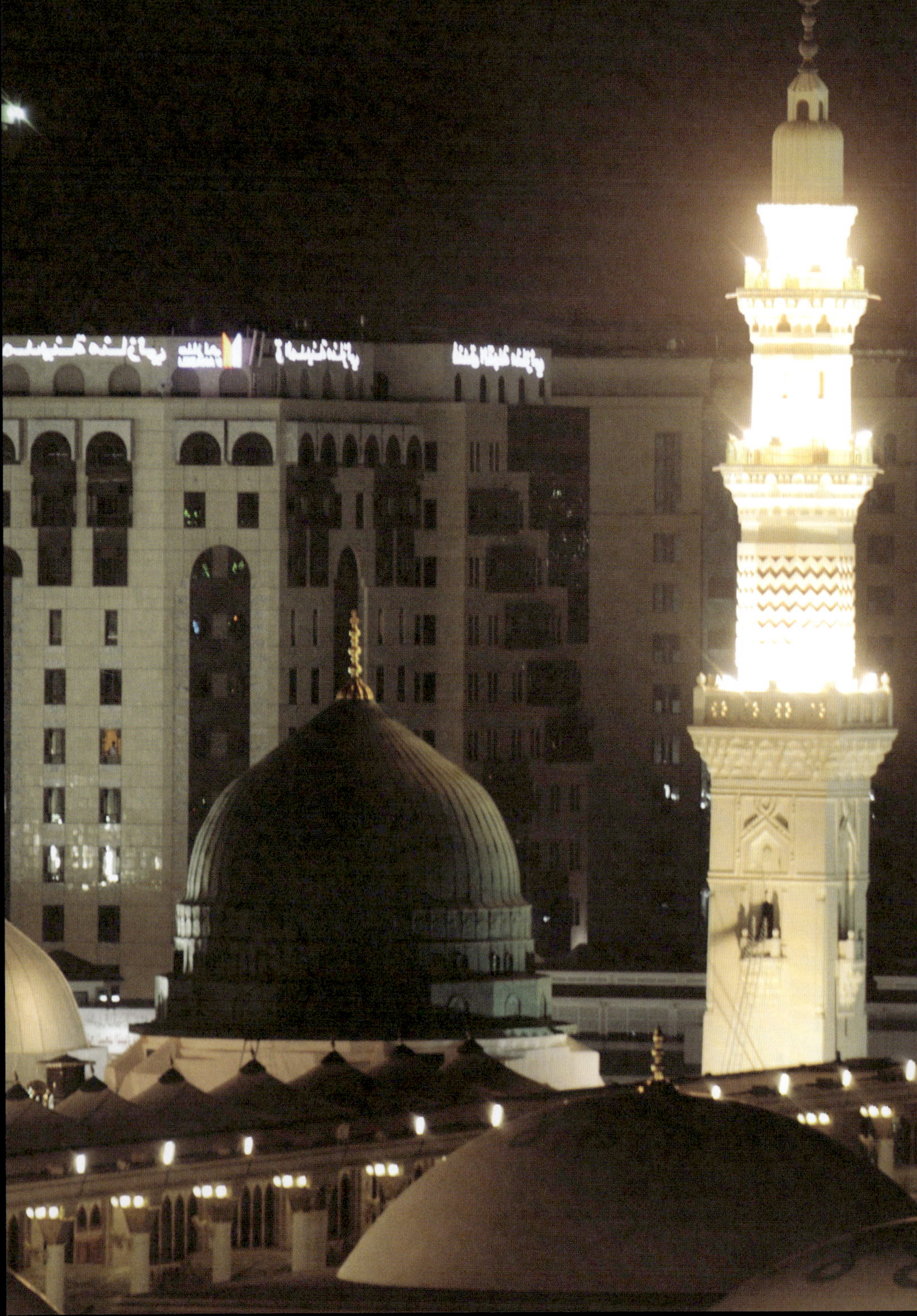

The Sunnah:
Celebrating
our Prophet by
following his example

Loving the beloved of Allah

Love for our Prophet Muhammad (peace be upon him), the last and final Messenger of Allah, is an essential part of our faith:

Say: "If your fathers, children, brothers, spouses, relatives and the wealth you have gathered, the business whose downturn you fear and the houses that delight you, if these things are dearer to you than Allah, His Messenger and struggling in His path, then you should wait until Allah's Judgement comes to pass. Allah doesn't guide the disobedient." (Qur'an 9:24)

Say: "If you love Allah then follow me, and Allah will love you and forgive your sins. Allah is the Forgiver, the Kind." (Qur'an 3:31)

The Prophet (peace be upon him) said, "None of you will have faith until he loves me more than his father, his children and all mankind." (Bukhari)

A man asked the Prophet (peace be upon him) about the Hour (i.e. Day of Judgement) saying, "When will the Hour be?" The Prophet (peace be upon him) said, "What have you prepared for it?" The man said, "Nothing, except that I love Allah and His Prophet." The Prophet (peace be upon him) said, "You will be with those whom you love." (Bukhari)

The most perfect role model

To increase our love for the Prophet (peace be upon him) we must learn about him and follow his example (Sunnah). This is why Allah says about His beloved in the Qur'an:

> You have an excellent role model in the Messenger of Allah, particularly for anyone who longs for Allah and the Last Day and remembers Him abundantly. (Qur'an 33:21)

Rewards for acting upon the Sunnah

Fortunately for us, the Prophet's family and companions (Sahabah — may Allah be pleased with them all) recorded every detail about his life. There is nothing hidden about him and there is no person in history about whom more is known.

The rewards for acting upon the example of the Prophet (peace be upon him) are immense, both in this life and the next:

The Prophet (peace be upon him) said: "Whoever revives my Sunnah, loves me. Whoever loves me will be with me in Jannah (Paradise)." (Tirmidhi)

The Prophet (peace be upon him) said: "Whoever revives an aspect of my Sunnah that is forgotten after my death, he will have a reward equivalent to that of the people who follow him, without it detracting in the least from their reward." (Tirmidhi)

The Prophet (peace be upon him) said: "Whoever adheres to my Sunnah when my Ummah is corrupt will have the reward of a hundred martyrs." (Al-Targheeb, Kitabuz Zuhd of Baihaqi, Al-Kamil of Ibn 'Adiy, Ibn Batta's Al-Ibanatul Kubra)

The excellent character of the Prophet

Given the excellent character of the Prophet (peace be upon him), when we follow his example our character and behaviour will also improve.

For example, Syedina Zaid ibn Haritha (may Allah be pleased with him), who grew up in the house of the Prophet (peace be upon him) says that in the 10 years he spent there as a child, never once did the Prophet (peace be upon him) show any displeasure at his misbehaviours.

The Prophet's wife, Syedatuna Aisha (may Allah be pleased with her) describes how the Prophet (peace be upon him) would help with the housework and play games and joke with her.

The companions of the Prophet (may Allah be pleased with them all) describe how, when he would talk to someone he would turn to face them completely and not turn away while the conversation was on-going. They would feel as if they were the most important person in the world for him due to the attention and love he directed towards them.

The Prophet was known as al-Amin ('the trustworthy one') and even after he revealed his Prophethood and the Quraysh became staunch enemies, they would entrust their property and goods in his care because they knew he had never lied, stolen or cheated.

He would enquire about and go out of his way to help not just his family and friends or those in need, but also those who verbally and physically abused him and tortured and even murdered his followers. He would forgive them even when he was in a position of power and able to take revenge (such as following the assault in Taif, and after conquering Makkah).

Dawah through action

This is the best form of Dawah (inviting others to Islam). The Prophet (peace be upon him) and his companions (may Allah be pleased with them all) had such excellent character that people would see their behaviour and when they realised that this was due to adherence to the teachings of Islam, they themselves wanted to become Muslims.

This is as true today as it was then; if we wish to convey the message of Islam to the people we know, the best way to do it is through our actions rather than our words. Unfortunately, for Muslims today the opposite is true; non-Muslims see our behaviour and want nothing to do with Islam. We need to change this and the best way is to follow the practices and develop the character of the Prophet (peace be upon him) within ourselves.

Our religion places a very high value on having a good character:

> *The Prophet (peace be upon him) said: "The most beloved of Allah's servants to Allah are those with the best manners." (Bukhari)*

> *The Prophet (peace be upon him) said: "Nothing is weightier on the Scale of Deeds than one's good manners." (Bukhari)*

Practical benefits

Following the way of the Prophet (peace be upon him) will not only help us in our spiritual development, enabling us to draw closer to Allah and His Prophet (peace be upon him), but will also help us in our everyday lives with the real-world problems that we all face. This is beautifully exemplified in the following story.

Syedina Abdullah bin Mubarak (may Allah be pleased with him) was born about 100 years after the Hijri (migration from Makkah to Madinah), and was involved in a battle where the Muslims had laid siege to a fort. Despite their efforts they could not break the siege. So they had a meeting where they came to the conclusion that there must be a practice of the Prophet (peace be upon him) they were not following which is why Allah had not granted them victory. However, they could not think of a single practice they were not fulfilling. So they sent a messenger to Madinah. The reply they received was to make sure they were doing Miswak (brushing their teeth with a toothbrush made from a twig). They immediately set to work cutting branches from the nearby trees to make their Miswak. A look-out on the fort was watching the Muslims and, horrified at what he was witnessing, fled to his commander. He told him that their only chance now was to surrender because the Muslims had started sharpening their teeth and were getting ready to eat them.

While the connection between following a nearly 1500-year-old practice and unrelated problems within our modern lives might seem very distant, we must remember that Allah is Musabib'al-Asbab – The Originator of Causes. Consider, how could anyone have predicted that the Muslim army using Miswak would help them conquer the fort but when Allah wants to create an opening for us then He does as He pleases, and He is Al-Qahhar (The Irresistible).

A word of warning

I must also mention a word of warning for those who consider the Sunnah of the Prophet (peace be upon him) to be unimportant or an unnecessary part of our religion. Allah told us quite clearly, through his Prophet (peace be upon him), that:

> *"Whoever turns away from my Sunnah, then they are not of me." (Bukhari)*

> *"The loss of religion begins with abandonment of Sunnah. Just as a rope breaks fibre by fibre, so does faith vanish with abandoning the principles of Sunnah, one by one." (Darimi)*

```
          Allah
            ↕
    Prophet Muhammad
            ↕
         Mankind
```

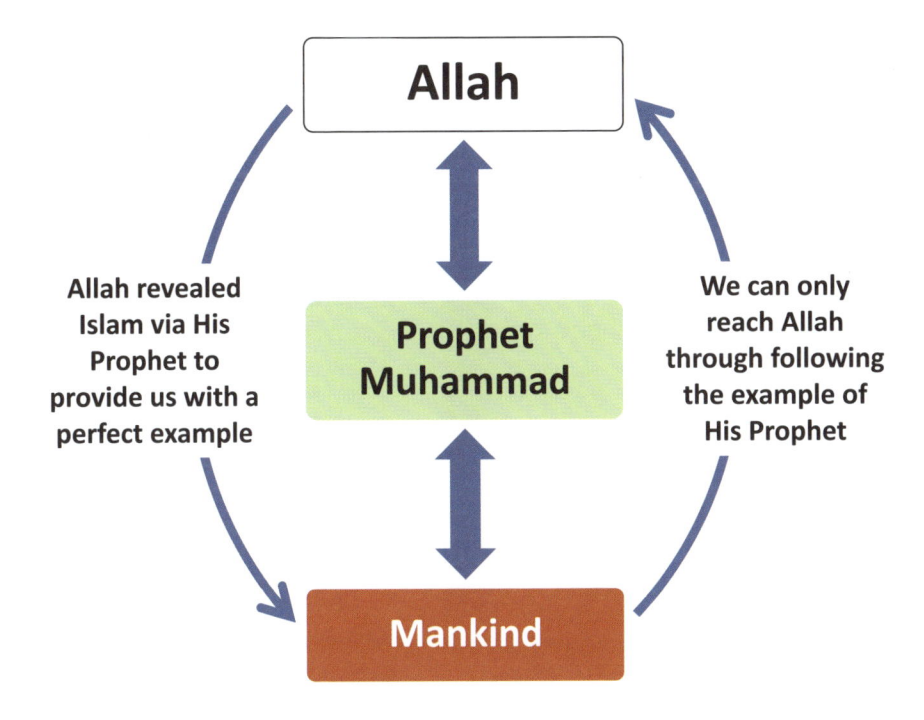

Allah revealed Islam via His Prophet to provide us with a perfect example

We can only reach Allah through following the example of His Prophet

Making a habit of following the Sunnah

This chapter contains a list of practices of the Prophet (peace be upon him), split into two groups; simple or small (often relating to actions), and larger or more complex (often relating to our emotions and character). The purpose is to choose practices to act upon and incorporate into our lives.

We should choose only one to begin with and then make a firm intention to try and incorporate it into our daily life, while praying to Allah for His help. There is space to record the date we make this intention and when it becomes second nature to us, record that date also and move onto a second practice.

We need to avoid the trap that the devil (Shaitan) will set for us; to pick many practices at the same time or to move too quickly from one practice to the next, because we will be more likely to fail and give up altogether. We should heed the advice of our Prophet (peace be upon him):

"Take up good deeds only as much as you are able, for the best deeds are those done regularly even if they are few." (Ibn Majah)

While doing this we should always remember why we are doing it. We are following the example of the Prophet (peace be upon him) to increase our love for him and draw closer to him as well as obeying the command of Allah and earning His pleasure. Having such a noble intention means that Allah will help us, as we are told in the Hadith Qudsi:

"He who draws close to Me a hand's span, I will draw close to him an arm's length. And whoever draws near Me an arm's length, I will draw near him a fathom's length. And whoever comes to Me walking, I will go to him running..." (Bukhari)

It is not my intention to include a complete list of Sunnah in this chapter (a near impossible task) but for it to serve as an introduction to develop this habit. Once we have exhausted the practices listed here we should have the desire and motivation to search for further practices to incorporate into our daily life. For this reason I have included several blank pages.

Drawing closer to Allah and His Prophet A Practical Guide

	Simple Sunnah that are easier to follow	Date started	Date habit formed
1	Greet any Muslim you meet by saying Assalamo-alaykum wa rahmatullah wa barakatuh (peace, mercy, and blessings of Allah be upon you)		
2	When you meet another Muslim shake their hand (if appropriate) with a smile		
3	When you sneeze say Alhumdolillah (all praise and thanks belong to Allah)		
4	When you hear a person sneeze say Alhumdolillah, reply Yarhamukallah (may Allah have mercy upon you)		
5	When entering your house mention the name of Allah (saying Bismillah or giving Salam, even if no-one is at home)		
6	Walk to the Mosque on foot (even if not the whole way, park further away than normal in a place that does not inconvenience the local community)		
7	Remove anything from the road which may cause others harm or difficulty		
8	Enter the Mosque with the right foot, leave with the left foot		

The Sunnah: Celebrating our Prophet by following his example

	Simple Sunnah that are easier to follow	Date started	Date habit formed
9	Stand in the first row in the Mosque, if there is space		
10	When joining any gathering sit wherever a place is found rather than causing others to have to move on your account		
11	When you hear the Adhan (call to prayer), answer it by repeating the Arabic phrases after the Muezzin		
12	Recite Ayat'al-Kursi (the throne verse: Qur'an 2:255) after the obligatory prayers		
13	Recite the Tasbih of Syedatuna Fatima (may Allah be pleased with her) after the obligatory prayers		
14	Send peace (Salam) and blessings (Darud) upon the Prophet (peace be upon him) before and after making Dua		
15	Do not waste water while doing Wudu, e.g. do not leave the tap running		
16	Use Miswak to brush your teeth when doing Wudu		
17	Perform Ghusl (a bath or shower) on Fridays		
18	Wear clean white clothes every Friday		

Drawing closer to Allah and His Prophet A Practical Guide

	Simple Sunnah that are easier to follow	Date started	Date habit formed
19	In general, but specifically on Fridays, send peace (Salam) and blessings (Darud) upon the Prophet (peace be upon him) in abundance		
20	Dress in a beautiful manner according to your means without being wasteful or having pride in your heart		
21	For men, keep a beard and trim it (minimum one fist length), and trim your moustache		
22	Keep your fingernails short (at a minimum cutting them every 40 days)		
23	Regularly shave underarm and pubic hair (at a minimum every 40 days)		
24	Attend the funeral prayer of fellow Muslims, even if you do not know them		
25	Eat with your right hand		
26	Do not eat food that is very hot (wait for it to cool down) and do not blow on it		
27	Recite the Tasmiyah (Bismillah) before eating		
28	Eat from the side of your plate that is in front of you		

The Sunnah: Celebrating our Prophet by following his example

	Simple Sunnah that are easier to follow	Date started	Date habit formed
29	Eat without leaving any leftovers (but do not overfill your plate to begin with)		
30	Finish all your food in a way that your plate and cutlery are left clean		
31	After eating (with your hands) lick your fingers		
32	Wash both hands before and after eating (up to the wrists) and gargle		
33	Drink while sitting down, not standing		
34	Drink in three breaths (sips or gulps), removing the cup from the mouth after each sip		
35	Do not drink directly from a jug or bottle, pour the contents into a glass first		
36	After eating or drinking, say Alhumdulillah (all praise and thanks belong to Allah)		
37	Eat with others, rather than alone, and do not leave the table until everyone has finished		
38	Take a walk after dinner		
39	Enter the toilet with the left foot and leave with the right foot		

	Simple Sunnah that are easier to follow	Date started	Date habit formed
40	Urinate while sitting (not standing)		
41	When wearing clothes or shoes begin with the right side; when taking off clothes or shoes begin with the left side		
42	Sit while dressing or undressing		
43	Avoid yawning, if you cannot stop yourself, cover your mouth with your hand and try to avoid making a sound		
44	Change into some other clothes (e.g. pyjamas) before going to sleep		
45	Brush your teeth before going to sleep		
46	Go to sleep in a state of Wudu		
47	Sleep on your right-hand side, do not sleep on your stomach		
48	On awakening rub your face and eyes with the palms of your hands		
49	Make your bed in the morning		
50	When struck by any calamity or misfortune, recite the Istirja (Inna lillahi wa inna ilaihi raji'oon - We belong to Allah and to Him we will return)		

The Sunnah: Celebrating our Prophet by following his example

	Complex Sunnah that will take time and effort	Date started	Date habit formed
1	Pray the five daily prayers		
2	Recite Surah Mulk (Qur'an 67) before sleeping		
3	Sleep immediately after the Isha Prayer		
4	Wake up for Tahajjud Prayer (pre-Fajr Prayer)		
5	Do not sleep straight after Fajr		
6	After praying Fajr sit in the Mosque (or on the prayer mat, at home, for women) until the Sun rises and then pray a further two units (Rak'ah) of Prayer (Ishraq)		
7	Recite a portion of Qur'an every day, no matter how little		
8	Read Qur'an with the translation/commentary (Tafsir) to gain understanding		
9	Spend some time every day in quiet seclusion, meditating and remembering Allah (Dhikr'Allah)		
10	Fast on Mondays and/or Thursdays		
11	Respect your elders, especially your parents, try to never get angry or annoyed with them		

	Complex Sunnah that will take time and effort	Date started	Date habit formed
12	Keep good relations with all your relatives, even the ones you do not get on with		
13	Show mercy and kindness to those who are younger than you		
14	Inquire about the welfare of your neighbours and treat them with kindness		
15	Be hospitable towards guests, regardless of how important or unimportant you consider them to be		
16	Visit Muslims when they are sick, even if you do not know them personally		
17	When eating, fill a third of your stomach with food, a third with drink, leaving a third empty		
18	Do not find fault with the food you eat		
19	Keep your gaze on the ground when walking		
20	Always keep a smile on your face		
21	Speak softly and politely at all times		

The Sunnah: Celebrating our Prophet by following his example

	Complex Sunnah that will take time and effort	Date started	Date habit formed
22	Turn to face whoever is talking to you and give them your full attention until the conversation is over		
23	Have a sense of humour that does not include hurting the feeling of others or lying		
24	Abstain from idle talk and if you have nothing good to say about someone or something, do not say anything at all		
25	Try to control your anger by doing the following: - Recite the Ta'awwudh (A`udhu billah) - Perform Wudu - If standing, sit down; if sitting, lie down		

Drawing closer to Allah and His Prophet A Practical Guide

	Other Sunnah that I will try to follow	Date started	Date habit formed
1			
2			
3			
4			
5			
6			
7			
8			
9			
10			
11			
12			

The Sunnah: Celebrating our Prophet by following his example

	Other Sunnah that I will try to follow	Date started	Date habit formed
13			
14			
15			
16			
17			
18			
19			
20			
21			
22			
23			
24			
25			

	Other Sunnah that I will try to follow	Date started	Date habit formed
26			
27			
28			
29			
30			
31			
32			
33			
34			
35			
36			
37			
38			

The Sunnah: Celebrating our Prophet by following his example

	Other Sunnah that I will try to follow	Date started	Date habit formed
39			
40			
41			
42			
43			
44			
45			
46			
47			
48			
49			
50			

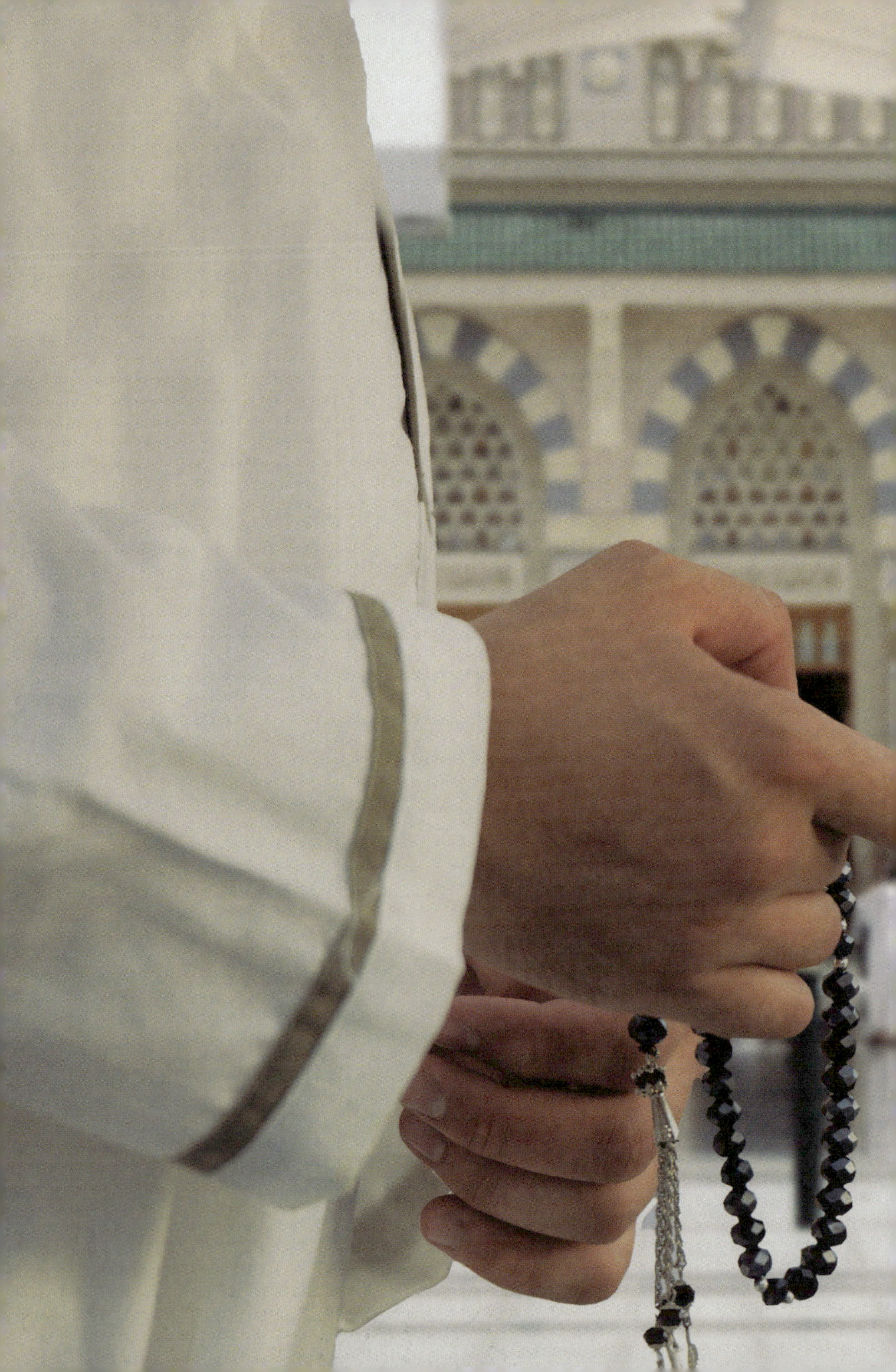

Sending peace and blessings upon the Prophet

Being in the company of Allah and His Angels

Allah and His angels continually bless the Messenger; so believers, you too bless and greet him with peace. (Qur'an 33:56)

In this verse Allah is instructing the believers to carry out two actions: to send blessings (Darud) and salutations/peace (Salam) upon the Prophet (peace be upon him).

> When this verse was revealed the Sahabah (may Allah be pleased with them all) asked the Prophet (peace be upon him), "O Messenger of Allah, we know how to convey Salam (i.e. what is read in the Atahiyyat – As-salamu alayka ayyhuha'n-nabiyyu wa rahmatu'llahi wa barakatuhu...), teach us how to convey blessings." The Prophet (peace be upon him) taught them, "Allahumma salli ala Muhammadinw wa ala ali Muhammad..." (i.e. Darud Ibrahimi that is read after Atahiyyat). (Bukhari)

The unique nature of sending peace and blessings upon the Prophet

As the above Hadith shows, not only does Allah command His believers to send peace and blessings upon the Prophet within the Qur'an, but He has also chosen to include this within the Salah. By doing this Allah is elevating its status and showing us its importance. We are also being told that sending peace and blessings upon the Prophet (peace be upon him) is in reality a form of Ibadah (worshipping Allah), since we are following His command.

This act is also unique because it is the only deed Allah has prescribed for us which He and His Angels are also participants in. Allah does not perform Salah, give charity, fast, or perform pilgrimage (Hajj), but He does send His peace and blessings upon His Prophet and He commands His Angels and His believers to do the same.

A supplication to Allah

It is important to clarify that even though Allah is asking us to send peace and blessings upon the Prophet (peace be upon him) that is not what we are doing. If we read the translation of any Salam or Darud (including Darud Ibrahimi) it is a Dua to Allah for Him to send peace and blessings upon the Prophet (peace be upon him). So how do we fulfil this command?

The explanation scholars have given for this is that for us to directly send peace and blessings upon the Prophet (peace be upon him) we would need to be higher in rank than him. Given the Prophet's status as the pinnacle of all creation and the most beloved of Allah, there is nothing within creation that is worthy of sending peace upon him or blessing him. Therefore, all of creation asks Allah to send His peace and His blessings upon His Prophet (peace be upon him) instead.

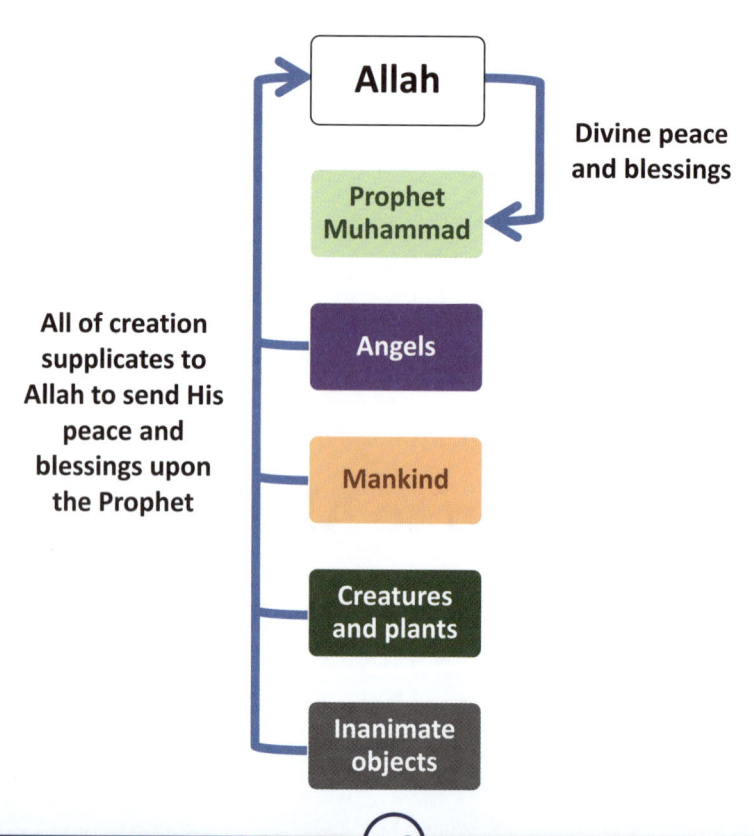

Divine peace and blessings

All of creation supplicates to Allah to send His peace and blessings upon the Prophet

- Allah
- Prophet Muhammad
- Angels
- Mankind
- Creatures and plants
- Inanimate objects

Love for our Prophet (peace be upon him)

Love for the Prophet (peace be upon him) is part of our faith:

Say: "If your fathers or your sons or your brothers or your wives or your tribe, or any wealth you have acquired, or any business you fear may slump, or any house which pleases you, are dearer to you than Allah and His Messenger and doing Jihad in His Way, then wait until Allah brings about His command. Allah does not guide people who are deviators." (Qur'an 9:24)

Say, "If you love Allah, then follow me and Allah will love you and forgive you for your wrong actions..." (Qur'an 3:31)

The Prophet (peace be upon him) said, "None of you will have faith until he loves me more than his father, his children and all mankind." (Bukhari)

A man asked the Prophet (peace be upon him) about the Hour (i.e. Day of Judgement) saying, "When will the Hour be?" The Prophet (peace be upon him) said, "What have you prepared for it?" The man said, "Nothing, except that I love Allah and His Prophet." The Prophet (peace be upon him) said, "You will be with those whom you love." (Bukhari)

Our Prophet (peace be upon him) is the one through whom Allah blessed us with Iman (faith). It is through his intercession that most of us will be saved from receiving punishment in Hell and enter Paradise. He was constantly remembering us and praying for our forgiveness throughout his prophethood, including when Allah brought him into His presence on the miraculous night journey (al-Isra w'al-Mi'raj), on his deathbed, and from his grave in Madinah.

> *The Prophet (peace be upon him) said, "My life is blissful for you because you hear traditions from people and relate them to others and my death is also blissful for you because your deeds will be presented to me. If I see the virtues prevail, I will be grateful to Allah, and if I see the vices prevail, I will pray for your forgiveness from Allah." (Bazzar)*

His love for us is obvious but if we truly love him as we claim to do, should we not also constantly remember him? One of the most powerful ways to express this love and to increase it further is to send peace and blessings upon him in abundance. The Prophet (peace be upon him) told us:

> *"Indeed, the person closest to me on the day of Judgement is he who invokes blessings upon me most abundantly." (Tirmidhi)*

Rewards for sending peace and blessings upon the Prophet

The Prophet (peace be upon him) told us that:

> *"The person in whose presence I am mentioned should invoke blessings upon me. Whoever invokes blessings upon me, Allah confers ten blessings upon him, forgives ten of his sins and elevates his status tenfold thereby."* (Ahmad)

It is impossible to put a value on even one of Allah's blessings, let alone ten. Indeed, one of His blessings is sufficient for His entire creation, let alone one of His servants. Furthermore, we have our sins forgiven and status raised, all in return for asking Allah to fulfil His own command of sending peace and blessings upon His Prophet (peace be upon him). These immeasurable rewards Allah bestows upon those who send peace and blessings is evidence of the depth of love Allah has for His Prophet (peace be upon him).

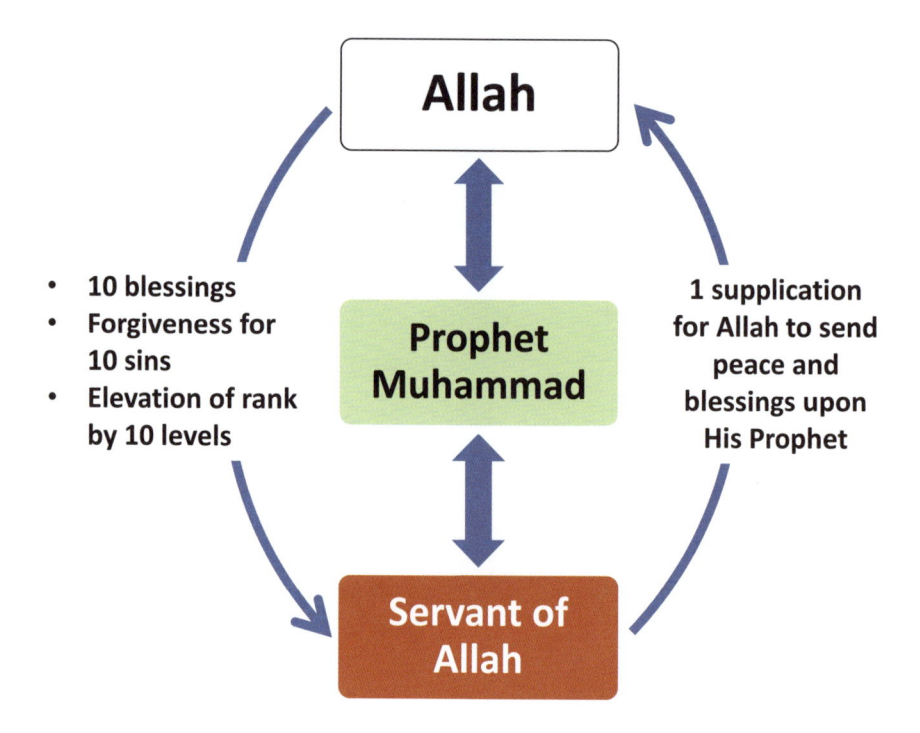

```
                    ┌─────────────┐
                    │    Allah    │
                    └─────────────┘
                           ↕
- 10 blessings       ┌─────────────┐      1 supplication
- Forgiveness for    │   Prophet   │      for Allah to send
  10 sins            │  Muhammad   │      peace and
- Elevation of rank  └─────────────┘      blessings upon
  by 10 levels              ↕             His Prophet
                    ┌─────────────┐
                    │  Servant of │
                    │    Allah    │
                    └─────────────┘
```

A warning

Unfortunately, there are some Muslims who believe that since this is not a compulsory act, it is of little importance. Leaving aside the Qur'anic injunction, and the fact that Salah itself cannot be performed without reciting peace and blessings upon the Prophet (peace be upon him), we are told that:

> *"Dua (supplication) is suspended between heaven and earth and none of it is taken up until you send blessings upon your Prophet (peace be upon him)." (Tirmidhi)*

There are also clear Hadith related to those who do not fulfil this command, especially upon hearing his name.

> One day, while the Prophet (peace be upon him) was ascending the three steps of the Minbar (pulpit) the companions (may Allah be pleased with them all) heard him say: "Ameen, Ameen, Ameen."
> They asked why he had done this. He replied: "Jibra'il came to me and said: 'May that person be destroyed who witnesses the month of Ramadan but is not forgiven.' I said 'Ameen.'
> Jibra'il then said: 'May that person be destroyed in whose presence you are mentioned but does not invoke blessings upon you.' I said 'Ameen.'
> Jibra'il then said: 'May that person be destroyed who finds both or one of his parents in old age, but they do not enter paradise.' I said 'Ameen.'" (ibn Hibban)

When, where, and how much?

This question was asked of the Prophet himself (peace be upon him) by one of his companions (may Allah be pleased with them all):

> "O Messenger of Allah, I wish to invoke blessings upon you abundantly, how much of my time set aside for supplication (Dua) should I devote to this purpose?"

The Prophet (peace be upon him) replied, "As much as you like."
He asked, "One quarter?"
The Prophet (peace be upon him) replied, "If you like, but if you do more it shall be better for you."
He asked, "One half?"
The Prophet (peace be upon him) replied, "If you like, but if you do more it shall be better for you."
He asked, "Two thirds?"
The Prophet (peace be upon him) replied, "If you like, but if you do more it shall be better for you."
So he said, "I shall devote all my time to invoke blessings upon you!"
The Prophet (peace be upon him) replied, "In that case, all your worries will be taken care of and your sins will be forgiven." (Tirmidhi)

We need not worry about where we are or what we are doing when we invoke peace and blessings upon the Prophet (peace be upon him); they are indeed being listened to and reach him:

> *"Allah has certain Angels who roam the earth and convey the greetings of my followers to me." (Nasai)*

> *"No person sends peace upon me except that Allah returns my soul to me, so that I may reply to him." (Abu Dawood)*

The numerous forms that peace and blessings upon the Prophet take

The simplest and shortest form of sending peace and blessings upon the Prophet (peace be upon him) is what is read upon hearing his name:- Sallallahu Alayhi Wasallam (peace be upon him) or Sallallahu Alayhi Wa'aalihi Wasallam (peace be upon him and his family and true followers).

The only Darud mentioned within the Hadith literature is Darud Ibrahimi, which is recited in Salah. However, there are hundreds of other Darud which we find within the Islamic literature. I have included the English translations of a few examples:

❖ **Darud-e-Shafi**

O Allah! Shower blessings on Muhammad whenever he is remembered by those who remember him, and shower blessings on Muhammad and his family whenever he is not remembered by the negligent.

❖ **Darud-e-Tanajeena**

O Allah! Shower blessings on Muhammad, our master, and his family and true followers such blessings by means of which You may relieve us of all anxieties and calamities; You may satisfy all our needs, You may clean us of all evils, and thanks for which You may grant us high position and high rank and status in Your presence, and You may lead us to the utmost limit of our aspirations and capacity in whatever is best in this world as well as in the Hereafter, as You have full power over everything.

❖ Darud-e-Nariya

O Allah! Every moment and in every breath, bestow complete and the best blessings and perfect peace which is endless on Muhammad, our master, and on his descendants and his companions, and may, for his sake, all our troubles and tortures be over, calamities ended, and all our needs fulfilled, all our cherished desires attained, and good-ends vouch-saved; and clouds are laden with water through the glorious countenance of the Prophet. The perfect blessings and peace on the Prophet's House, his family and his companions every instance in number equal to the count of all things in Your knowledge.

❖ Darud-e-Qur'ani

O Allah! Send Your blessings and peace on Muhammad, our master, and on his family and companions according to the number of every letter in the Qur'an and let each letter carry thousands of blessings and salutations in it.

So a question naturally arises as to where these Darud came from? The answer is that they are gifts which the pious, the Awliyah-Allah, the true lovers of the Prophet have been given. They are often received within dreams and then shared with the rest of us, or composed as acts of love and then afterwards accepted by the Prophet (peace be upon him) within dreams. Four very famous examples are given below.

Tanam Farsuda Jaan Para

Mawlana Abdur Rahman Jami (may Allah have mercy upon him) had composed a poem in Farsi – 'Tanam Farsuda Jaan Para', when he decided to go on pilgrimage to Makkah with the intention to stand at the grave of the Prophet (peace be upon him) and recite the verses he had composed.

When he set out for Madinah the governor of Makkah saw the Prophet (peace be upon him) in a dream, telling him to stop Mawlana Jami from entering Madinah. The governor at once set his agents to work, and when Mawlana Jami tried to enter Madinah he was turned away. But given his strong yearning to visit the Prophet (peace be upon him) he tried a different route.

Once again the governor of Makkah had a dream in which the Prophet (peace be upon him) told him that this man was still trying to enter Madinah and must be stopped. Again, the governor set his agents to work, and this time, when they found Mawlana Jami, they arrested him.

Yet again that night the governor had a dream in which the Prophet (peace be upon him) came to him, this time telling him that the man they arrested was not a criminal but one of his lovers who had composed poetry. If he was to enter Madinah and recite it at his grave the Prophet (peace be upon him) would extend his hand out of his grave to shake Mawlana Jami's hand and this would cause great confusion.

Dala'il al-Khayrat

The 'Dala'il al-Khayrat' is another great work of love for the Prophet (peace be upon him) written by Imam Jazuli (may Allah have mercy upon him). One day while in Khalwa (solitary retreat) Imam Jazuli went to perform Wudu from a nearby well but could not find any means to draw the water up.

While searching nearby he was seen by a young girl who called out, "You're the one people praise so much and you cannot even figure out how to get water out of a well?" She spat into the water, which welled up until it overflowed.

Imam Jazuli made his Wudu and then turned to her and said, "I ask you to tell me how you reached this rank?" She replied, "By saying blessings upon him whom the beasts lovingly followed as he walked through the jungles." Imam Jazuli (may Allah have mercy upon him) thereupon vowed to compose the book of blessings on the Prophet that came to be known as his 'Dala'il al-Khayrat'.

Balaghal-ula be-Kamal-e-hi

When Shaykh Saadi Shirazi (may Allah have mercy upon him) was composing 'Balaghal-ula be-Kamal-e-hi' he couldn't think of what to write for the final verse. While working on it, one night as he slept, he found himself in the blessed presence of the Prophet (peace be upon him) and his companions (may Allah be pleased with them all).

The Prophet (peace be upon him) asked him what was disturbing him, why he looked troubled. Shaykh Saadi replied that he had composed a Rubai (a four lined Persian poem) for the Prophet but could not finish it. The Prophet (peace be upon him) asked him to recite it and upon hearing the first three lines, himself added the final line, 'Sallu alae-hi wa Aal-e-hi.'

Qaseeda Burda Sharif

The 'Qaseeda Burda Sharif' (the mantle ode) was written by Imam Busiri (may Allah have mercy upon him), who was known for the poems he would write in praise of the Prophet (peace be upon him). During his lifetime he suffered a stroke which paralysed half of his body. He was seen by the physicians of the time but no cure was found and as time passed he began to lose hope.

In desperation Imam Busiri composed one more poem in love of the Prophet (peace be upon him) and also requested the Prophet to intercede for him and supplicate for Allah to cure him. He repeatedly sang the poem, wept, prayed, and asked for intercession.

When he slept, in his dream he saw the Prophet (peace be upon him) who wiped Imam Busiri's face with his blessed hands and covered him in his mantle/cloak (Burdah). When Imam Busiri (may Allah have mercy upon him) awoke, he found that he was able to walk, so he got up and left his house.

He had told no one about what had happened but on the way encountered one of the Awliyah-Allah who said to him: "I want you to give me the poem in which you praise the Prophet (peace be upon him)." Imam Busiri asked which one, given that he was known as a writer of poetry in love of the Prophet (peace be upon him). But the saint replied, "The one that you composed during your sickness."

Before Imam Busiri could answer, the saint recited the first verse and said: "I swear by Allah that I heard it in a dream last night being sung in the presence of the Prophet Muhammad (peace be upon him). I saw the Prophet was pleased with it and covered the person who sang it with his cloak." So Imam Busiri (may Allah be pleased with him) realised it was Allah's will for this poem to be made public.

Making a habit of sending peace and blessings upon the Prophet

In summary, we should strive to make sending peace and blessings upon the Prophet second nature for us; in doing so love for the Prophet will blossom in our hearts, we will draw closer to him, and we may even be so blessed as to receive our very own Darud as a gift.

The purpose of this chapter is to provide a practical means of developing this habit. We should set ourselves a weekly goal of how many peace and blessings we want to send upon the Prophet (peace be upon him) and then try and accomplish this by daily recitation. There are tables on the following pages to record our progress.

We need to avoid the trap the devil will set for us, to set the goal too high and in doing so, make things difficult for ourselves. We will be more likely to fail and abandon the habit before it becomes established. Instead we should start small and gradually increase the number we read each day/week, remembering the words of our Prophet (peace be upon him):

> *"Take up good deeds only as much as you are able, for the best deeds are those done regularly even if they are few."* (ibn Majah)

In this way sending peace and blessings upon the Prophet (peace be upon him) will become easy for us and a part of our daily routine. We should have this noble intention from the very beginning and make Dua to Allah for help in this struggle. As we are told in the Hadith Qudsi:

> *"He who draws close to Me a hand's span, I will draw close to him an arm's length. And whoever draws near Me an arm's length, I will draw near him a fathom's length. And whoever comes to Me walking, I will go to him running..." (Bukhari)*

Sending peace and blessings upon the Prophet

Weekly goal (number of Salam and Darud to send upon the Prophet)			
Day	**Number**	**Day**	**Number**
Friday		Tuesday	
Saturday		Wednesday	
Sunday		Thursday	
Monday		**Weekly total**	

Weekly goal (number of Salam and Darud to send upon the Prophet)			
Day	**Number**	**Day**	**Number**
Friday		Tuesday	
Saturday		Wednesday	
Sunday		Thursday	
Monday		**Weekly total**	

Weekly goal (number of Salam and Darud to send upon the Prophet)			
Day	**Number**	**Day**	**Number**
Friday		Tuesday	
Saturday		Wednesday	
Sunday		Thursday	
Monday		**Weekly total**	

Weekly goal (number of Salam and Darud to send upon the Prophet)			
Day	**Number**	**Day**	**Number**
Friday		Tuesday	
Saturday		Wednesday	
Sunday		Thursday	
Monday		**Weekly total**	

Weekly goal (number of Salam and Darud to send upon the Prophet)			
Day	**Number**	**Day**	**Number**
Friday		Tuesday	
Saturday		Wednesday	
Sunday		Thursday	
Monday		**Weekly total**	

Weekly goal (number of Salam and Darud to send upon the Prophet)			
Day	**Number**	**Day**	**Number**
Friday		Tuesday	
Saturday		Wednesday	
Sunday		Thursday	
Monday		**Weekly total**	

Sending peace and blessings upon the Prophet

Weekly goal			
(number of Salam and Darud to send upon the Prophet)			
Day	**Number**	**Day**	**Number**
Friday		Tuesday	
Saturday		Wednesday	
Sunday		Thursday	
Monday		**Weekly total**	

Weekly goal			
(number of Salam and Darud to send upon the Prophet)			
Day	**Number**	**Day**	**Number**
Friday		Tuesday	
Saturday		Wednesday	
Sunday		Thursday	
Monday		**Weekly total**	

Weekly goal			
(number of Salam and Darud to send upon the Prophet)			
Day	**Number**	**Day**	**Number**
Friday		Tuesday	
Saturday		Wednesday	
Sunday		Thursday	
Monday		**Weekly total**	

Drawing closer to Allah and His Prophet A Practical Guide

Weekly goal (number of Salam and Darud to send upon the Prophet)			
Day	**Number**	**Day**	**Number**
Friday		Tuesday	
Saturday		Wednesday	
Sunday		Thursday	
Monday		**Weekly total**	

Weekly goal (number of Salam and Darud to send upon the Prophet)			
Day	**Number**	**Day**	**Number**
Friday		Tuesday	
Saturday		Wednesday	
Sunday		Thursday	
Monday		**Weekly total**	

Weekly goal (number of Salam and Darud to send upon the Prophet)			
Day	**Number**	**Day**	**Number**
Friday		Tuesday	
Saturday		Wednesday	
Sunday		Thursday	
Monday		**Weekly total**	

Sending peace and blessings upon the Prophet

Weekly goal (number of Salam and Darud to send upon the Prophet)			
Day	**Number**	**Day**	**Number**
Friday		Tuesday	
Saturday		Wednesday	
Sunday		Thursday	
Monday		**Weekly total**	

Weekly goal (number of Salam and Darud to send upon the Prophet)			
Day	**Number**	**Day**	**Number**
Friday		Tuesday	
Saturday		Wednesday	
Sunday		Thursday	
Monday		**Weekly total**	

Weekly goal (number of Salam and Darud to send upon the Prophet)			
Day	**Number**	**Day**	**Number**
Friday		Tuesday	
Saturday		Wednesday	
Sunday		Thursday	
Monday		**Weekly total**	

Drawing closer to Allah and His Prophet A Practical Guide

Weekly goal (number of Salam and Darud to send upon the Prophet)			
Day	**Number**	**Day**	**Number**
Friday		Tuesday	
Saturday		Wednesday	
Sunday		Thursday	
Monday		**Weekly total**	

Weekly goal (number of Salam and Darud to send upon the Prophet)			
Day	**Number**	**Day**	**Number**
Friday		Tuesday	
Saturday		Wednesday	
Sunday		Thursday	
Monday		**Weekly total**	

Weekly goal (number of Salam and Darud to send upon the Prophet)			
Day	**Number**	**Day**	**Number**
Friday		Tuesday	
Saturday		Wednesday	
Sunday		Thursday	
Monday		**Weekly total**	

Sending peace and blessings upon the Prophet

Weekly goal (number of Salam and Darud to send upon the Prophet)			
Day	**Number**	**Day**	**Number**
Friday		Tuesday	
Saturday		Wednesday	
Sunday		Thursday	
Monday		**Weekly total**	

Weekly goal (number of Salam and Darud to send upon the Prophet)			
Day	**Number**	**Day**	**Number**
Friday		Tuesday	
Saturday		Wednesday	
Sunday		Thursday	
Monday		**Weekly total**	

Weekly goal (number of Salam and Darud to send upon the Prophet)			
Day	**Number**	**Day**	**Number**
Friday		Tuesday	
Saturday		Wednesday	
Sunday		Thursday	
Monday		**Weekly total**	

Weekly goal (number of Salam and Darud to send upon the Prophet)				
Day	**Number**	**Day**	**Number**
Friday		Tuesday	
Saturday		Wednesday	
Sunday		Thursday	
Monday		**Weekly total**	

Weekly goal (number of Salam and Darud to send upon the Prophet)				
Day	**Number**	**Day**	**Number**
Friday		Tuesday	
Saturday		Wednesday	
Sunday		Thursday	
Monday		**Weekly total**	

Weekly goal (number of Salam and Darud to send upon the Prophet)				
Day	**Number**	**Day**	**Number**
Friday		Tuesday	
Saturday		Wednesday	
Sunday		Thursday	
Monday		**Weekly total**	

Sending peace and blessings upon the Prophet

Weekly goal (number of Salam and Darud to send upon the Prophet)			
Day	**Number**	**Day**	**Number**
Friday		Tuesday	
Saturday		Wednesday	
Sunday		Thursday	
Monday		**Weekly total**	

Weekly goal (number of Salam and Darud to send upon the Prophet)			
Day	**Number**	**Day**	**Number**
Friday		Tuesday	
Saturday		Wednesday	
Sunday		Thursday	
Monday		**Weekly total**	

Weekly goal (number of Salam and Darud to send upon the Prophet)			
Day	**Number**	**Day**	**Number**
Friday		Tuesday	
Saturday		Wednesday	
Sunday		Thursday	
Monday		**Weekly total**	

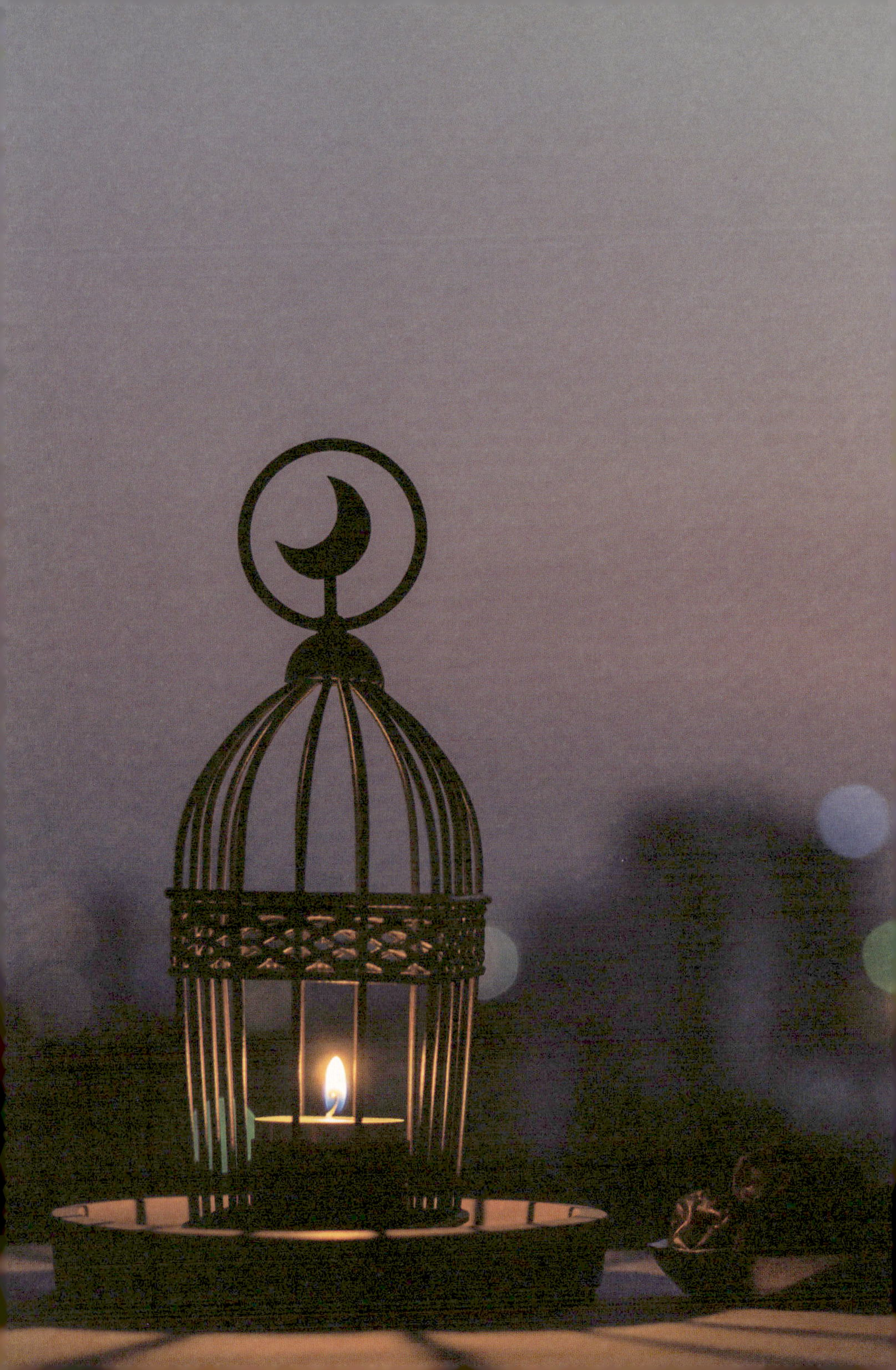

Fasting: Training our Nafs and increasing our Taqwa

Islam – the universal religion from the beginning of time

It is a common misconception that Islam began with the Prophet Muhammad (peace be upon him). In actual fact Islam (translated as 'submission to the will of Allah') is the true religion of all Prophets, from the Prophet Adam to the Prophet Muhammad (peace be upon them all).

As human society developed over time so did their relationship with Allah until revelation of the perfected religion to the final Messenger, the 'Seal of the Prophets' (peace be upon him):

> *Today, I have completed your religion for you; I gave My favour in full, and I am pleased that Islam is your religion. (Qur'an 5:3)*

Humans have always fasted as a form of worship

Every previous Prophet was given forms of worship that involved fasting (Siyam):

> *Believers, fasting has been compulsory for you as it was made compulsory for those before you so you become mindful of Allah. (Qur'an 2:183)*

Even now if we look at the Jews and the Christians we find forms of fasting prescribed within their books and practiced by the pious amongst them.

What does fasting involve?

Fasting is not eating and drinking from sunrise to sunset. This makes us experience what it is like to be hungry or thirsty. It allows us to empathise with those who are in such a state because they have nothing to eat or drink, sometimes for days at a time.

This should have two results: to increase our gratitude to Allah for all that He has blessed us with, and increase the charity we give to the poor and needy. We have failed to benefit from this aspect of fasting if we overcompensate for the thirst and hunger we feel during the day by overeating during the night.

The Prophet (peace be upon him) said, "If a person does not refrain from lying and indecent activities, Allah does not want that he should abstain from eating and drinking." (Bukhari)

Fasting is not just a prohibition on eating and drinking but also all other major and minor sins including bad habits which have become like second nature to so many of us (lying, backbiting, arguing, cheating, stealing, fighting – especially with family, friends, neighbours, and the wider community at large).

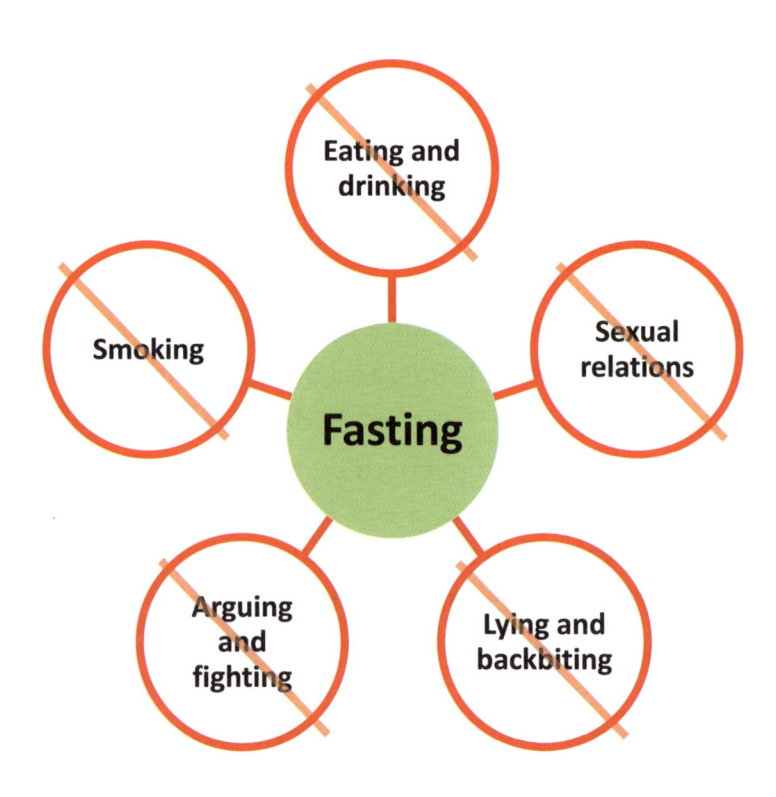

Fasting prohibits:
- Eating and drinking
- Sexual relations
- Lying and backbiting
- Arguing and fighting
- Smoking

Taqwa – consciousness of Allah

In the above Qur'anic verse, we are told that fasting is a means of becoming mindful of Allah (developing 'Taqwa'). A more complete translation would be to change our behaviour due to consciousness and fear of the consequences of displeasing Allah. This is developed through a realisation that Allah is always watching us and has complete knowledge of everything we say and do.

When someone is watching us, even if it is someone we do not know, we are very careful about what we say or do. If it is a friend or relative, we are even more careful; we do not want them to see us engaged in bad behaviour that is shameful. Imagine then, if our mosque's Imam was with us, or our Shaykh (spiritual teacher); we would be on our best behaviour.

So then consider, that it is none other than Allah, the Lord of the universe, the King of kings, and our Creator, who is always watching us, who knows our every deed. If we truly believed this, would we be able to partake in any sinful act?

One of the Awliyah Allah said, "Consider not the insignificance of sin you are about to commit, instead consider the greatness of the One you are about to disobey."

The blessed month of Ramadan and its connection to the Qur'an

One of the most blessed months in the Islamic calendar is Ramadan, a month in which fasting is obligatory and ends with the celebration of Eid'al-Fitr:

> *The Quran was revealed in the month of Ramadan; the Quran is a guidance for people, it contains clear teachings and distinguishes right from wrong; whoever is present in the month must fast in it, but, if anyone is ill or on a journey, then let them fast an equivalent number of days later. Allah wants ease for you, not difficulty, and wants to see you complete the compulsory number of fasts. So, glorify Allah for guiding you, and be ever-thankful. (Qur'an 2:185)*

The blessings of this month are linked to the final Revelation of Allah, the Qur'an, revealed to His final Prophet and Messenger, Muhammad (peace be upon him):

> *We sent down the Quran on the Night of Destiny, and what can explain the Night of Destiny to you? The Night of Destiny is better than one thousand months, the Angels and the Spirit, Jibra'il, come down by the order of their Lord, bringing with them each person's*

destiny. Peace descends everywhere until the break of the dawn. (Qur'an 97)

This blessed night is worth more than a thousand months, equivalent to over 83 years of worship. Scholars have debated whether this was the night when the entirety of the Qur'an was sent down from al-Lauh al-Mahfuz (the preserved tablet – in which is recorded everything that has ever happened and will ever happen), to the lowest Heaven, from where it was revealed to the Prophet (peace be upon him) over 23 years via the Archangel Jibra'il (may Allah be pleased with him), or the night when the Archangel came to the Prophet with the first Revelation of the Qur'an:

Recite in the name of your Lord Who created...
(Qur'an 96:1)

Consider then, the significance of the Qur'an, the uncreated speech of Allah, that on the night of its descent Allah bestows rewards equivalent to a lifetime of worship on those of His servants who search for it within the last ten nights of Ramadan.

Our two enemies – the Nafs and Shaitan

The Prophet (peace be upon him) said, "When the month of Ramadan starts, the doors of Heaven are opened and

> *the gates of Hell are closed and the Shayatin (Devils) are chained." (Bukhari)*

If the devil and his helpers (Shayatin) are unable to whisper to us, why do we commit sins in Ramadan? This is because we follow our Nafs. This is the untrained part of our soul/self which produces 'animal' desires within us; to eat, drink, sleep, find comfort, be lazy, lust and procreate; whether by Halal or Haram means. This is the Nafs al-Ammara ('the commanding soul/self'):

> *...since human ego continually incites one to do evil, except when My Lord is kind to me. My Lord is Forgiving, Kind. (Qur'an 12:53)*

It is through encouraging the untrained Nafs that the devil encourages us to indulge ourselves and sin; discouraging us from putting in the effort to perform good deeds. If we let this Nafs take over and follow its every desire then we are no better than animals, in fact we are worse because they have no choice but to act upon their instincts, whereas we have a degree of self-control, and therefore, choice.

Training of the Nafs

Training our self is essential to decrease the influence it has upon us and to lessen our inclination to follow the whispers of the devil. By doing this the Nafs al-Ammara develops into the

Nafs al-Lawwamah ('the blaming/self-reproaching soul/self'), which feels guilty whenever it disobeys Allah and commits sins, and encourages us to seek forgiveness:

...and I swear by the self-critical soul! (Qur'an 75:2)

This is not easy; in fact, it is very difficult to remain engaged in such a struggle for our whole life. Once the Prophet (peace be upon him) was returning from the battlefield with his Sahabah (may Allah be pleased with them all) when he told them they were going from the lesser Jihad (al-Jihad al-Asghar) to the greater Jihad (al-Jihad al-Akbar). The Sahabah (may Allah be pleased with them all) were puzzled, what could be a greater Jihad than on the battlefield? The Prophet (peace be upon him) told them that Jihad (literally translated as 'to struggle' or 'to strive') against your own self is even more difficult than being willing to sacrifice your life on the battlefield.

The path to peace

Training of the self was practiced by all the Awliyah-Allah. Whenever their Nafs desired anything they purposefully denied it; be that food, drink, sleep, good clothes, or any other comfort of this world. These are not things which are impermissible, but to gain proximity to Allah we have to continuously deny the pleasures of this world to become indifferent to them.

These saints would often leave civilisation at some point in their lives, wandering in the jungles and deserts, literally leaving the world behind and learning to rely entirely on Allah. When they returned to humanity, they were a means for Allah to benefit His creation. They were able to live in the world but not be of it, since their self was firmly under their control. At this stage, the Nafs al-Lawwamah has become the Nafs al-Mutma'inna ('the peaceful soul/self'):

> *Allah will say: O happy soul! Return to Your Lord cheerfully and loved. (Qur'an 89:27-28)*

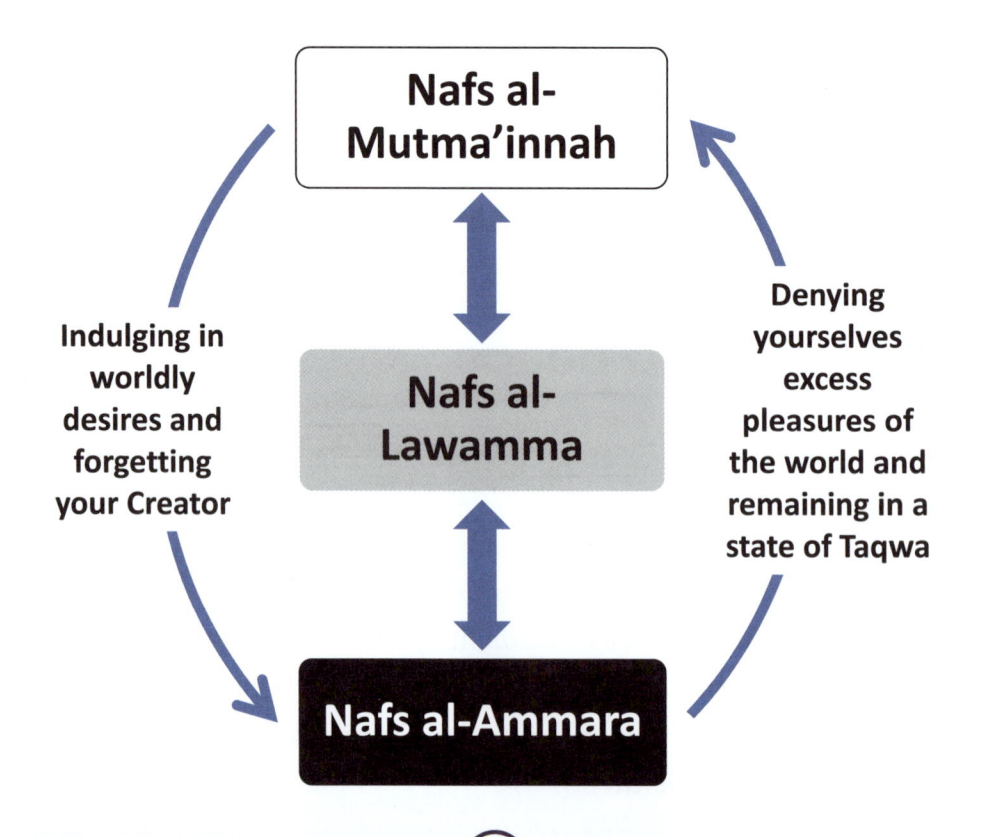

Nafs al-Mutma'innah

Nafs al-Lawamma

Nafs al-Ammara

Indulging in worldly desires and forgetting your Creator

Denying yourselves excess pleasures of the world and remaining in a state of Taqwa

Taking advantage of our opportunities

So in this blessed month of obligatory fasting we have an annual opportunity to develop our Taqwa and to train our untrained self by distancing ourselves from the world and turning our attention towards our Lord and Creator.

This is done by trying to pray for longer with greater concentration (Khushu) because we are less distracted by worldly thoughts and desires, by giving away our wealth in charity to those less fortune than ourselves and by abstaining even from eating and drinking.

The immense and immeasurable rewards of fasting

The many teachings of the Prophet (peace be upon him) related to the blessings and rewards associated with fasting, make clear how much Allah loves this act of worship.

> *The Prophet (peace be upon him) said: "Whoever fasts during Ramadan out of sincere faith and hoping to attain Allah's rewards, then all his past sins will be forgiven." (Bukhari)*

The Prophet (peace be upon him) was asked: 'O Messenger of Allah, tell me of an action by which I may enter Paradise." He (peace be upon him) said: "Take to fasting, there is nothing like it." (Nasai)

The Prophet (peace be upon him) said, "On the Day of Judgement, fasting will say: "O My Lord, I prevented him from food and desires so accept my intercession for him.""" (Ahmad)

The Prophet (peace be upon him) said, "Fasting is a shield with which a servant protects himself from the Fire." (Ahmad)

The Prophet (peace be upon him) said, "...Allah has made fasting during it (Ramadan) an obligation, and steadfastly observing its nights in worship a voluntary act. Whoever undertakes an act of obedience to Allah during this month with a voluntary good deed, it is as if he has performed an obligatory act at other times; and whoever performs an obligatory act during it is as one who performed seventy obligations at other times. It is the month of patience, and the reward for patience is Paradise. It is the month of goodwill, during which provisions are multiplied. Whoever feeds a fasting person will be compensated with forgiveness of sins and salvation of his soul from Hell. He will also receive

> *a reward equal to that of the person he feeds, without causing him any reduction (in his good deeds)." (Bayhaqi)*
>
> *The Prophet (peace be upon him) said, "Every action of the son of Adam is given manifold reward, each good deed receiving 10 times its like, up to seven hundred times. Allah the Most High said, 'Except for fasting, for it is for Me and I will give recompense for it, he leaves off his desires and his food for Me.' For the fasting person there are two times of joy; a time when he breaks his fast and a time of joy when he meets his Lord, and the smell coming from the mouth of the fasting person is better to Allah than the smell of musk." (Bukhari)*

So within this blessed month the devil and his helpers are chained and Allah has multiplied the already countless blessings He bestows upon us. We fast the entire month, the pleasures of which are twofold; once experienced upon opening the fast and the other upon the Day of Judgement, when Allah will reward the believer Himself. Within the last ten nights Allah has also included the hidden gem of Laylat'al-Qadr (the night of power/decree):

> *"The Prophet (peace be upon him) said, "Whoever establishes the prayers on the Night of Qadr out of sincere faith, and hoping to attain Allah's rewards, then all his past sins will be forgiven." (Bukhari)*

Erasure of a lifetime of (minor) sins

Allah is so merciful that He is looking for any excuse to forgive His slaves, and so the Prophet (peace be upon him) told us about specific acts of worship or times within the year when we have these opportunities (the most famous example of which is the pilgrimage to Makkah – Hajj, which actually leads to forgiveness of all major and minor sins).

These opportunities come every year, having spent Ramadan training our untrained self, increasing our consciousness of Allah, our old sins are washed away, ready to make a fresh start and lead the kind of pious lives we aspire to. However, Allah knows His creation is weak. We often start well but as time passes we fall back into our bad habits, and so He has given us this blessed month and this blessed night every year.

Fasting outside of Ramadan

Fasting as an act of worship is not confined to Ramadan, we can achieve its blessings at other times of the year, specifically those mentioned below.

❖ Six fasts of Shawwal

In the month following Ramadan (Shawwal), it is a Sunnah to fast for six days. These can be kept at any time during the month and not necessarily consecutively. Regarding these six fasts the Prophet (peace be upon him) said:

> *"Whoever fasts Ramadan and follows it with six days from Shawwal it is as if they fasted the entire year." (Muslim)*

This is clarified by the following Hadith:

> *"Allah has made for each Hasanah (good deed) ten like it, so a month is like fasting ten months, and fasting six days completes the year." (Nasai)*

If we are able to do this every year then the following Hadith would apply to us:

> *The Messenger of Allah (peace be upon him) said: "Whoever fasts Ramadan and follows it with six days of Shawwal, it will be as if he fasted for a lifetime." (Ibn Majah)*

Consider standing before Allah on the Day of Judgement with a lifetime of fasts upon our scale, the reward for which Allah has said He, Himself will give.

❖ Ten days and nights of Dhul Hijja

Regarding the first ten days and nights of Dhul Hijjah (the 12th and final month in the Islamic calendar), Allah says in the Qur'an:

> *By the dawn, by the ten holy nights... (Qur'an 89:1-2)*

The Prophet (peace be upon him) said:

> *"There are no other days that are as great as these in the sight of Allah, the Most Sublime. nor are there any deeds more beloved to Allah than those that are done in these ten days..." (Tabarani)*

In his Hadith commentary (Fath al-Bari), Ibn Hajar al-Ascalani (may Allah have mercy upon him) explained:

> *"The most apparent reason for the ten days of Dhul Hijjah being distinguished in excellence is due to the assembly of the greatest acts of worship in this period, i.e. Salawat (Prayers), Siyam (fasting), Sadaqah (charity) and the Hajj (pilgrimage). In no other periods do these great deeds combine."*

❖ Day of Arafat (the 9th of Dhul Hijja)

The day of Arafat is on the 9th of Dhul Hijja. From sunrise until sunset, all of the pilgrims stand in prayer before Allah. The Prophet (peace be upon him) said, "The best of supplications are those on the Day of Arafat," (Tirmidhi) and that, "Hajj is Arafat." (Tirmidhi)

In another Hadith he said, "There is no day on which Allah frees more of His slaves from Jahannam (fire of Hell) than the Day of Arafat..." (Muslim) and, "Verily Allah boasts of the people of Arafat before the people of Heaven (i.e. the Angels) saying: 'Look to my servants who have come to Me dishevelled and dusty.'" (Ahmad)

But the mercy of Allah is such that His blessings are not only reserved for those performing the pilgrimage (Hajis). For the rest of us the Prophet (peace be upon him) said: "Fasting on the day of Arafat is an expiation (forgiveness of sins) for two years, the year preceding it and the year following it." (Ibn Majah)

❖ The month of Sha'ban

Sha'ban is the month preceding Ramadan, in which the Prophet (peace be upon him) prepared for the coming month by fasting frequently:

> *Syedatuna Aisha (may Allah be pleased with her) said, "I did not see the Messenger of Allah fast any month in its entirety except Ramadan, and I did not see him fast as frequently in any other month as he did during Sha'ban." (Bukhari)*

> The Prophet (peace be upon him) was asked, "I have never seen you offer fast in a month as you do in Sha'ban." To which he replied, "It is a month people disregard that is between Rajab and Ramadan. In that month deeds are presented to the Lord of the Worlds, so I like my deeds to be presented while I am fasting." (Nasai)

❖ Laylat'al-Bara'ah (the night of the 15th of Sha'ban)

As indicated in the following Hadith there are specific blessings associated with the night of the 15th of Sha'ban (Laylat'al-Bara'ah):

> The Prophet (peace be upon him) said, "When the middle night of Sha'ban arrives, you should stand (praying) in the night and should fast in the day following it." (Ibn Majah)

> The Prophet (peace be upon him) said, "Allah turns to His entire creation on the fifteenth night of Sha'ban and forgives all of them except one who ascribes partners to Him and one who harbours enmity in his heart." (Tabarani)

It is for this reason that this blessed night is called Laylat'al-Bara'ah – which means the night wherein judgement of salvation from Hell is passed.

❖ The night of the Isra w'al-Mi'raj

The Isra w'al-Mi'raj is the name of the miraculous night journey the Prophet (peace be upon him) was taken on, from Makkah to al-Aqsa Mosque and from there into the presence of Allah. Given the unique nature and immeasurable blessings of Allah upon His Prophet (peace be upon him), and through him to his Ummah (community of followers), this is an event that Muslims have celebrated through the ages.

It is believed to have occurred on the night of the 27th of Rajab (the month before Sha'ban — Imam Nawawi stated this in his Rawdah, and Imam Ghazali maintained this opinion in his Ihya' 'Ulum al-Din — may Allah have mercy upon them both).

Celebrations involve gatherings at local Mosques to listen to religious talks and Nasheed (religious songs), and partake in sending peace and blessings upon the Prophet (peace be upon him), and fasting the next day. However, there are no Hadith to support this act as a Sunnah, therefore it is done as means of expressing gratitude to, and worshipping Allah.

❖ The day of Ashura (the 10th of Muharram)

When the Prophet (peace be upon him) arrived in Madinah he found that the Jews there fasted on the 10th of Muharram (the first month in the Islamic calendar) and asked them the reason for this. They said, "This is a blessed day. On this day Allah saved the Children of Israel from their enemy (in Egypt) and so Prophet Moses fasted on this day giving thanks to Allah." The Prophet (peace be upon him) said, "We are closer to Moses than you are." (Muslim)

With regards the blessings associated with this fast:

> *The Prophet (peace be upon him) said, "Fasting the day of Ashura (is of great merits), I hope that Allah will accept it as an expiation for (the sins committed in) the previous year." (Muslim)*

The Prophet (peace be upon him) advised to fast for two days rather than just on the 10th of Muharram (i.e. the 9th and 10th, or 10th and 11th). The scholars give two reasons for this; to differentiate ourselves from the Jews, and to make sure we do not miss the fast of the 10th due to uncertainty over moon-sighting indicating the start of the month.

❖ Fasting on Mondays and Thursdays and three days every month

> *The Prophet (peace be upon him) said: "Deeds are shown (to Allah) on Mondays and Thursdays, and I like my deeds to be shown when I am fasting." (Tirmidhi)*

The Prophet (peace be upon him) was asked about fasting on Mondays and he said: "On (that day) I was born and on it Revelation came down to me." (Muslim)

The Messenger of Allah (peace be upon him) said. "If you fast any part of the month then fast on the thirteenth, fourteenth and fifteenth." (Ahmad)

❖ **The fasting of the Prophet David (peace be upon him)**

The Prophet (peace be upon him) said: "The best fasting is the fast of David (peace be upon him) ... he used to fast one day and not the next." (Bukhari)

Making a habit of fasting throughout the year

The purpose of this chapter is to help develop a habit of fasting both inside and outside of Ramadan. Reading the above should have shown the immense blessings associated with this special form of worship.

However, to take advantage of this we have to remember that fasting is not solely to do with staying hungry and thirsty from sunrise to sunset, it must also involve abstinence from all sins and an effort to increase our good deeds, both regarding the creation and the Creator. Only with that intention will we start to gain control over our untrained self and increase our consciousness of Allah, thereby emptying our heart from the love of this world and replacing it with the true love of Allah.

On the following pages I have included tables to record our fasting throughout the year. We need to avoid the trap that the devil will set for us, to try to do too much too quickly because we will be more likely to fail.

> **The Prophet (peace be upon him) said, "Take up good deeds only as much as you are able, for the best deeds are those done regularly even if they are few." (Ibn Majah)**

While doing this, we should always remember why we are doing it. Make Dua to Allah for help in this struggle, remembering the Hadith Qudsi:

> *"He who draws close to Me a hand's span, I will draw close to him an arm's length. And whoever draws near Me an arm's length, I will draw near him a fathom's length. And whoever comes to Me walking, I will go to him running..." (Bukhari)*

Fasting: Training our Nafs and increasing our Taqwa

Ramadan Fast	Did I fast today?	Did I pray 5 times today?	Did I perform Tirawi Prayer?	Did I recite Quran today?	Did I overeat at Iftar?	Did I abstain from other sins?
1	Yes/No	Yes/No	Yes/No	Yes/No	Yes/No	Yes/No
2	Yes/No	Yes/No	Yes/No	Yes/No	Yes/No	Yes/No
3	Yes/No	Yes/No	Yes/No	Yes/No	Yes/No	Yes/No
4	Yes/No	Yes/No	Yes/No	Yes/No	Yes/No	Yes/No
5	Yes/No	Yes/No	Yes/No	Yes/No	Yes/No	Yes/No
6	Yes/No	Yes/No	Yes/No	Yes/No	Yes/No	Yes/No
7	Yes/No	Yes/No	Yes/No	Yes/No	Yes/No	Yes/No
8	Yes/No	Yes/No	Yes/No	Yes/No	Yes/No	Yes/No
9	Yes/No	Yes/No	Yes/No	Yes/No	Yes/No	Yes/No
10	Yes/No	Yes/No	Yes/No	Yes/No	Yes/No	Yes/No

Drawing closer to Allah and His Prophet A Practical Guide

Ramadan Fast	Did I fast today?	Did I pray 5 times today?	Did I perform Tirawi Prayer?	Did I recite Quran today?	Did I overeat at Iftar?	Did I abstain from other sins?
11	Yes/No	Yes/No	Yes/No	Yes/No	Yes/No	Yes/No
12	Yes/No	Yes/No	Yes/No	Yes/No	Yes/No	Yes/No
13	Yes/No	Yes/No	Yes/No	Yes/No	Yes/No	Yes/No
14	Yes/No	Yes/No	Yes/No	Yes/No	Yes/No	Yes/No
15	Yes/No	Yes/No	Yes/No	Yes/No	Yes/No	Yes/No
16	Yes/No	Yes/No	Yes/No	Yes/No	Yes/No	Yes/No
17	Yes/No	Yes/No	Yes/No	Yes/No	Yes/No	Yes/No
18	Yes/No	Yes/No	Yes/No	Yes/No	Yes/No	Yes/No
19	Yes/No	Yes/No	Yes/No	Yes/No	Yes/No	Yes/No
20	Yes/No	Yes/No	Yes/No	Yes/No	Yes/No	Yes/No

Fasting: Training our Nafs and increasing our Taqwa

Ramadan Fast	Did I fast today?	Did I pray 5 times today?	Did I perform Tirawi Prayer?	Did I recite Quran today?	Did I overeat at Iftar?	Did I abstain from other sins?
21	Yes/No	Yes/No	Yes/No	Yes/No	Yes/No	Yes/No
22	Yes/No	Yes/No	Yes/No	Yes/No	Yes/No	Yes/No
23	Yes/No	Yes/No	Yes/No	Yes/No	Yes/No	Yes/No
24	Yes/No	Yes/No	Yes/No	Yes/No	Yes/No	Yes/No
25	Yes/No	Yes/No	Yes/No	Yes/No	Yes/No	Yes/No
26	Yes/No	Yes/No	Yes/No	Yes/No	Yes/No	Yes/No
27	Yes/No	Yes/No	Yes/No	Yes/No	Yes/No	Yes/No
28	Yes/No	Yes/No	Yes/No	Yes/No	Yes/No	Yes/No
29	Yes/No	Yes/No	Yes/No	Yes/No	Yes/No	Yes/No
30	Yes/No	Yes/No	Yes/No	Yes/No	Yes/No	Yes/No

Six fasts of Shawwal	
What is the last day of this month (before which I need to keep the six fasts)?	
How many fasts did I keep?	1 / 2 / 3 / 4 / 5 / 6

Ten days/nights of Dhul Hijja	
What date did the first day of Dhul Hijja fall on?	
How many fasts did I keep?	
Did I fast on the day of Arafat (9th Dhul Hijja)?	Yes / No

Ashura – 10th of Muharram	
Did I fast on the 9th of Muharram?	Yes / No
Did I fast on the 10th of Muharram?	Yes / No
Did I fast on the 11th of Muharram?	Yes / No

Laylat'al-Bara'ah - 15th of Shaban	
What date does the 15th of Sha'ban fall on?	
Did I fast on the 15th of Sha'ban?	Yes / No

Charity: Investing in this life and the next

	Month:	
Did I fast on the 1st Monday?		Yes / No
Did I fast on the 1st Thursday?		Yes / No
Did I fast on the 2nd Monday?		Yes / No
Did I fast on the 2nd Thursday?		Yes / No
Did I fast on the 3rd Monday?		Yes / No
Did I fast on the 3rd Thursday?		Yes / No
Did I fast on the 4th Monday?		Yes / No
Did I fast on the 4th Thursday?		Yes / No
Did I fast on the 13th/14th/15th?		Yes / No

	Month:	
Did I fast on the 1st Monday?		Yes / No
Did I fast on the 1st Thursday?		Yes / No
Did I fast on the 2nd Monday?		Yes / No
Did I fast on the 2nd Thursday?		Yes / No
Did I fast on the 3rd Monday?		Yes / No
Did I fast on the 3rd Thursday?		Yes / No
Did I fast on the 4th Monday?		Yes / No
Did I fast on the 4th Thursday?		Yes / No
Did I fast on the 13th/14th/15th?		Yes / No

	Month:	
Did I fast on the 1st Monday?		Yes / No
Did I fast on the 1st Thursday?		Yes / No
Did I fast on the 2nd Monday?		Yes / No
Did I fast on the 2nd Thursday?		Yes / No
Did I fast on the 3rd Monday?		Yes / No
Did I fast on the 3rd Thursday?		Yes / No
Did I fast on the 4th Monday?		Yes / No
Did I fast on the 4th Thursday?		Yes / No
Did I fast on the 13th/14th/15th?		Yes / No

	Month:	
Did I fast on the 1st Monday?		Yes / No
Did I fast on the 1st Thursday?		Yes / No
Did I fast on the 2nd Monday?		Yes / No
Did I fast on the 2nd Thursday?		Yes / No
Did I fast on the 3rd Monday?		Yes / No
Did I fast on the 3rd Thursday?		Yes / No
Did I fast on the 4th Monday?		Yes / No
Did I fast on the 4th Thursday?		Yes / No
Did I fast on the 13th/14th/15th?		Yes / No

Charity: Investing in this life and the next

	Month:	
Did I fast on the 1st Monday?		Yes / No
Did I fast on the 1st Thursday?		Yes / No
Did I fast on the 2nd Monday?		Yes / No
Did I fast on the 2nd Thursday?		Yes / No
Did I fast on the 3rd Monday?		Yes / No
Did I fast on the 3rd Thursday?		Yes / No
Did I fast on the 4th Monday?		Yes / No
Did I fast on the 4th Thursday?		Yes / No
Did I fast on the 13th/14th/15th?		Yes / No

	Month:	
Did I fast on the 1st Monday?		Yes / No
Did I fast on the 1st Thursday?		Yes / No
Did I fast on the 2nd Monday?		Yes / No
Did I fast on the 2nd Thursday?		Yes / No
Did I fast on the 3rd Monday?		Yes / No
Did I fast on the 3rd Thursday?		Yes / No
Did I fast on the 4th Monday?		Yes / No
Did I fast on the 4th Thursday?		Yes / No
Did I fast on the 13th/14th/15th?		Yes / No

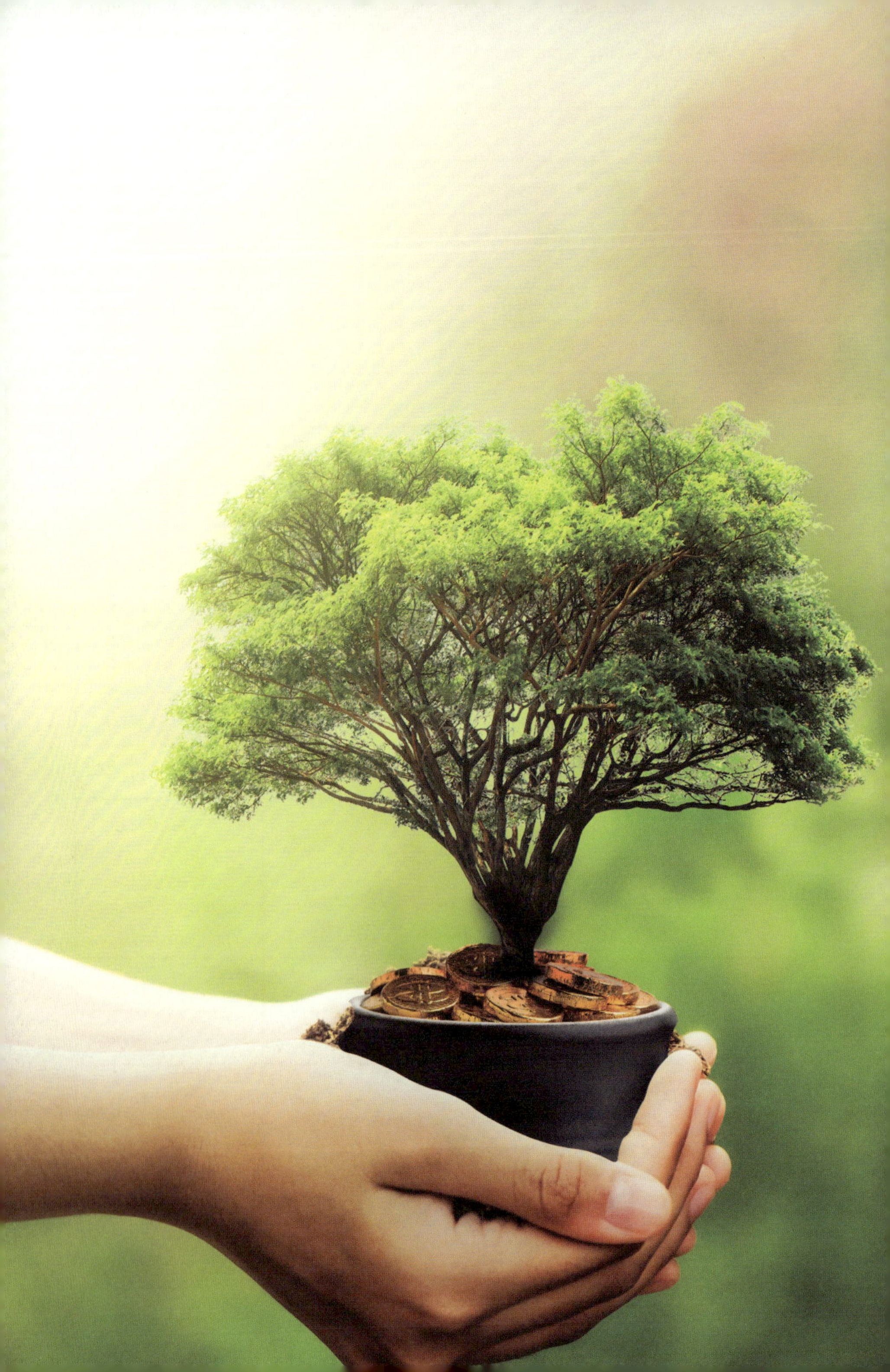

Charity: Investing in this life and the next

Sadaqah and Zakat

In Islam there is both obligatory and voluntary charity. Obligatory charity is known as Zakat and is one of the five pillars of Islam. It involves giving 2.5% of the wealth we own in charity every year (as long as it is above the 'Nisab' – a threshold value, we are an adult of sane mind and free from debt). The importance of this is such, that Allah mentions Zakat together with Salah no less than 82 times in the Qur'an:

> *...I shall decree what is good for those who are mindful of Me, pay Zakat and believe in Our signs. (Qur'an 7:156)*

> *...establish the prayer regularly, pay the Zakat and give Allah a beautiful loan. Remember, whatever good you stock up is for yourselves; in the Hereafter you will find it with Allah. You will be greatly rewarded... (Qur'an 73:20)*

The wisdom of Allah behind linking these two seemingly different acts of worship is because they both involve spending some of what Allah has given us in His way (our time for the Salah, and our wealth for Zakat). Apart from Zakat (which is obligatory) giving voluntary charity (Sadaqah) is also a very important part of our faith.

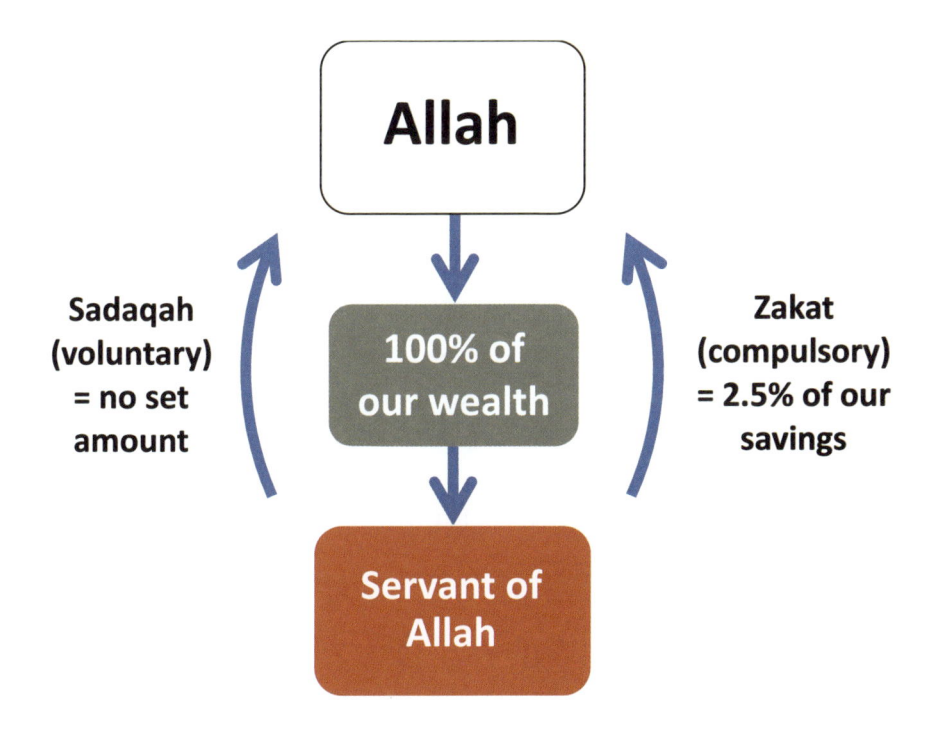

Allah

Sadaqah (voluntary) = no set amount

100% of our wealth

Zakat (compulsory) = 2.5% of our savings

Servant of Allah

The reality of giving charity

We must realise that Allah does not need our money. Indeed, the people or cause we are giving charity to also do not need our money. Allah is Ar-Razzaq (The Provider) and Ar-Raziq (The Sustainer) and He does not depend on our charity to fulfil His Divine attributes. As He says in the Qur'an:

> *Control of the Heavens, the Earth, and whatever lies within them belongs to Allah, and He has power over all things. (Qur'an 5:120)*

Therefore, when we give charity we should be clear that we are only helping ourselves. We must realise that Allah is the One who has given us everything we have and just because we have some wealth in our possession, it does not mean we are its owner. Everything we have, including our health, our wealth, our families, is a 'trust' from Allah. It is given to us for a period of time but it remains His and it is His to take back whenever He pleases and in whatever manner He pleases.

So is He not merciful then, that He gives us so much wealth and then asks for only a fraction of it to be spent in his way so that we can become the means (Sabab) by which He provides for His creation, and if we do this He is pleased with us?

The rewards for spending our wealth in Allah's way

> *Those people who spend their wealth in Allah's way are like a grain that sprouts into seven ears, each ear has a hundred seeds, and Allah will multiply it for them many times more as He pleases. Allah is The Vast, The Knowing. (Qur'an 2:261)*

Whatever good things you give in charity will benefit yourselves; that is, if you give, seeking only Allah's pleasure. Whatever good things you give in charity will be rewarded, and you will be not short-changed in the least. (Qur'an 2:272)

People who give their wealth in charity by night or by day, secretly or openly, shall have their reward from their Lord: they shall neither fear nor grieve. (Qur'an 2:274)

The Prophet (peace be upon him) said: "Charity finishes sins as water extinguishes fire." (Tirmidhi)

The Prophet (peace be upon him) said: "Give charity without delay, for it stands in the way of calamity." (Tirmidhi)

The Prophet (peace be upon him) said: "Charity cools the wrath of Allah and prevents a bad death." (Tirmidhi)

The Prophet (peace be upon him) said: "The believer's shade on the Day of Resurrection will be his charity." (Tirmidhi)

Given the immeasurable rewards mentioned in these Qur'anic verses and Hadith, could there be a better investment than to spend the wealth Allah has blessed us with in charity?

Fear of poverty

A sign of weak faith (Iman) is to be miserly when giving charity because we believe we will become poor as a result. This is impossible:

> *The Prophet (peace be upon him) said: "Charity does not in any way decrease the wealth..." (Muslim)*

> *The Prophet (peace be upon him) said: "Allah said: 'Spend, O son of Adam, and I shall spend on you.'" (Bukhari)*

As a reward for giving charity Allah may give us more wealth in this life, maybe immediately or in the future. Indeed, Allah may have given us the very wealth we are giving from because He knew we would give charity from it. Furthermore, our remaining wealth will have Barakah in it (it will be blessed so it will grow and increase). As such, even from a financial point of view the investment with the best guaranteed return is to give charity:

> *Who will offer Allah a loan, a beautiful loan, He will multiply its reward many times over. Allah withholds His favour, or He gives plenty, and to Him you will return. (Qur'an 2:245)*

Making sure our charity is not rejected

There are two important points we need to consider to ensure the charity we give is acceptable to Allah. The first is to make sure the money from which we are giving is not earned through Haram means.

> *The Prophet (peace be upon him) said, "A slave (of Allah) who acquires Haram wealth and gives charity from it, it is not accepted from him. If he spends from it, he does not have any blessing (Barakah) in it. If he leaves it behind him (i.e. he dies) it will be a means of taking him to the fire (of Hell). Verily, Allah does not wipe out an evil deed with an evil deed..." (Ahmad)*

For example, charity will not be accepted from money earned through sale of goods which are impermissible (e.g. alcohol, pig meat, prostitution), even if it is to non-Muslims. Similarly, the owner of a disco, nightclub or brothel, who is earning money from a business which encourages impermissible acts will not have their charity accepted. Business owners will not have their charity accepted if the money they make involves unfair or unjust practices with regards to how their workers are treated or paid. Similarly, people in a position of power e.g. police, military, political leaders, rulers of countries, will not be able to use money they have obtained through corruption, bribery or other unjust means. Obviously, any earning of money which involves lying, cheating or stealing is impermissible.

Such things will not apply to most of us, however, there are other, subtler pitfalls we should all be mindful of regarding our earnings. For example, if we consistently arrive to work late or leave early, even by five minutes, that results in part of our earnings becoming impermissible. If we waste time while at work (e.g. excessive talking to colleagues, taking frequent bathroom breaks which we do not need, coming back from break/lunch late, taking longer to do something that we could do much quicker), the same applies.

Not only will charity not be accepted from such earnings, but consider that we are then spending that money on buying food for ourselves and our family about which the Prophet (peace be upon him) said:

> *"No meat (i.e. person) that was nourished with Haram will enter Paradise. Every meat (i.e. person) that was nourished with Haram is more deserving of the Fire." (Ahmad)*

A common complaint we have is that our Dua are not accepted, but is this not then to be expected?

> *The Prophet (peace be upon him) made mention of a man who is constantly in journeys and has dishevelled hair and a dusty appearance (due to constant journeys for*

performing acts of righteousness such as Hajj, Umrah, seeking knowledge etc.) and he raises his hands towards the sky saying "O my Lord! O my Lord!" But his food is from Haram. His drink is from Haram. His clothes are from Haram. He is nourished from Haram. How can it (his supplication) be accepted? (Muslim)

The second condition is if our intention is to show off, so that people talk about us and praise us for our generosity. This raises the question of whether we should give charity openly or secretly. We should not assume that people who give charity openly are doing so to show off. If the intention is to inspire others to follow their example, this is a praiseworthy act. However, if we think that by giving charity openly, when others praise us we may start to enjoy their praise and become proud, it is better to give charity in secret:

> *If you give charity openly, that is wonderful, but giving it secretly to the needy is even better; in both cases it will compensate for your sins. Allah is fully aware of what you do. (Qur'an 2:271)*

> *"There are seven whom Allah will shade in His Shade on the Day when there is no shade except His Shade... one who gives in charity and hides it, such that his left hand does not know what his right hand gives in charity..." (Bukhari)*

Following on from this, once we have given charity we should forget about it and never remind those who we have given to. As Allah says in the Qur'an:

> *Those who spend their wealth in the way of Allah and do not follow it up by reminding the recipients of the favour, or causing them offence, shall have reward from their Lord: they shall neither fear nor grieve. (Qur'an 2:262)*

This is especially important when we give charity to those we know, be it family or friends. If people we know are in need they are more deserving of our money than people we do not know in a far-off country:

> *"The best charity is that which is practiced by a wealthy person. And start giving first to your dependents." (Bukhari)*

Indeed, even spending on our own family can be an act of charity:

> *The Prophet (peace be upon him) said: "When a Muslim spends something on his family intending to receive Allah's reward, it is regarded as charity for him." (Bukhari)*

Non-financial acts of charity

How can those who may not have much money, e.g. students, single parents, workers on minimum wage, give charity? The

Prophet (peace be upon him) was asked the very same question by his Sahabah (may Allah be pleased with them all):

> The Prophet (peace be upon him) said: "Every Muslim has to give in charity."
> The people then asked: "(But what) if someone has nothing to give, what should he do?"
> The Prophet (peace be upon him) replied: "He should work with his hands and benefit himself and also give in charity (from what he earns)."
> The people further asked: "If he cannot find even that?"
> He replied: "He should help the needy who appeal for help."
> Then the people asked: "If he cannot do (even) that?"
> The Prophet said finally: "Then he should perform good deeds and keep away from evil deeds, and that will be regarded as charitable deeds." (Bukhari)

> Some people from amongst the companions (may Allah be pleased with them all) said to the Prophet (peace be upon him), "O Messenger of Allah, the rich people have made off with the rewards; they pray as we pray, they fast as we fast, and they give [much] in charity by virtue of their wealth."
> The Prophet (peace be upon him) said, "Has not Allah made things for you to give in charity? Truly every Tasbeehah [saying: 'Subhan'Allah'] is a charity, and every Takbeerah [saying: 'Allahu Akbar'] is a charity, and every Tahmeedah [saying: 'Alhumdolillah'] is a charity, and

every Tahleelah [saying: 'La Illaha Ill'Allah'] is a charity. And commanding the good is a charity, and forbidding an evil is a charity, and in the sexual act of each one of you there is a charity."

The Sahabah (may Allah be pleased with them all) said, "O Messenger of Allah, when one of us fulfils his carnal desire, will he have some reward for that?"

The Prophet (peace be upon him) said, "Do you not see that if he were to act upon his desire in an unlawful manner then he would be deserving of punishment? Likewise, if he were to act upon it in a lawful manner then he will be deserving of a reward." (Muslim)

The mercy of Allah is so overwhelming that any act of worship (Ibadah), indeed any Halal act can be considered an act of charity and is rewarded accordingly:

"Every act of goodness is charity." (Muslim)

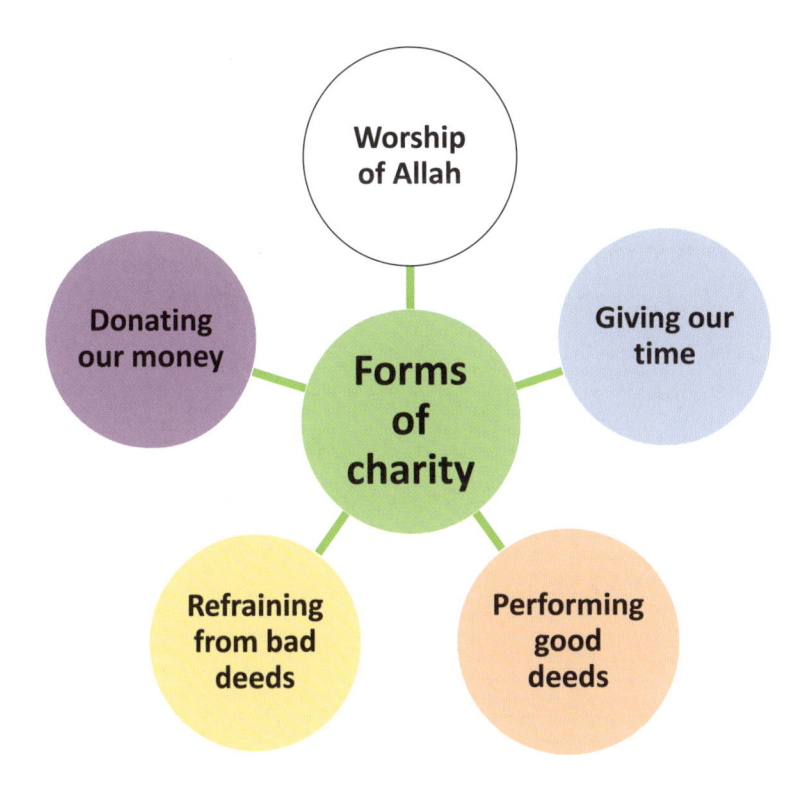

Forms of charity:
- Worship of Allah
- Giving our time
- Performing good deeds
- Refraining from bad deeds
- Donating our money

Gaining reward even after death

Charity is one of the few acts that can benefit us after our death, as the Prophet (peace be upon him) said:

> "When a slave dies his actions come to an end except three things: a continuing charity (Sadaqah Jariya), or knowledge which gives benefit, or a pious child who prays for him." (Muslim)

When we spend our money, time, or effort to do good or stop evil, as long as the effects of that continue, even after our death, we will continue to gain reward.

> *"Among the acts and good deeds that will reach a believer after his death are: knowledge which he learned and then spread; a righteous son whom he leaves behind; a copy of the Qur'an that he leaves as a legacy; a mosque that he built; a house that he built for wayfarers; a canal that he dug; or charity that he gave during his lifetime when he was in good health. These deeds will reach him after his death."* (Ibn Majah)

Therefore, apart from making sure we live a righteous life by following the commandments of Allah and example of the Prophet (peace be upon him), what more valuable investment can we make than regularly giving charity? The returns will help us at a time when there will be no further opportunity to do good deeds, no other way to earn the pleasure of Allah and be saved from His wrath.

Developing a habit of regular giving

The purpose of this chapter is to provide a practical means of developing the habit of giving charity. We should think about whether there are any family members, relatives, close friends or neighbours who are in financial difficulty. They have the first right to our money.

We should consider our local Mosque from which we gain such benefit and which runs entirely on the donations of its congregation.

We should think about poor Muslims within the UK, a significant number of whom are homeless or under debt – there are charities which help support them in this difficult time.

Other charities carry out projects in the poorest parts of the world (e.g. sponsoring orphans, building schools, digging wells) and in places where natural disasters or wars have caused immense suffering.

We might not be directly involved in Dawah (spreading the religious teachings of Islam), but these initiatives require financial support (e.g. radio/TV channels, local/national organisations).

We should consider whether we would prefer to make a single donation or set up a monthly standing order, remembering the words of the Prophet (peace be upon him):

> *"Take up good deeds only as much as you are able, for the best deeds are those done regularly even if they are few." (Ibn Majah)*

We need to avoid the trap the devil will set for us, to give too much too quickly and cause ourselves financial difficulty. We will be more likely to regret what we have done and abandon the habit before it becomes established.

Instead we should start small and gradually increase the number and amount of our donations, keeping in mind that any act of kindness to others (even animals) and all forms of worship are counted as charity.

We can use the blank tables on the following pages for record our progress. By regularly reviewing our charitable acts and donations we will gradually develop a habit of giving and helping others, it will become part of our daily routine. We should have this noble intention from the very beginning and make Dua to Allah for help in this struggle. As we are told in the Hadith Qudsi:

> *"He who draws close to Me a hand's span, I will draw close to him an arm's length. And whoever draws near Me an arm's length, I will draw near him a fathom's length. And whoever comes to Me walking, I will go to him running..." (Bukhari)*

The Divine Decree: Finding peace through acceptance

Month	
Are there any family members, relatives, friends or neighbours going through financial difficulty?	Yes / No
Am I supporting my local Mosque?	Yes / No
Which Dawah projects am I supporting?	
Where in the world am I helping those in need?	
What Sadaqah Jariya projects am I involved in?	

Month	
Are there any family members, relatives, friends or neighbours going through financial difficulty?	Yes / No
Am I supporting my local Mosque?	Yes / No
Which Dawah projects am I supporting?	
Where in the world am I helping those in need?	
What Sadaqah Jariya projects am I involved in?	

Month	
Are there any family members, relatives, friends or neighbours going through financial difficulty?	Yes / No
Am I supporting my local Mosque?	Yes / No
Which Dawah projects am I supporting?	
Where in the world am I helping those in need?	
What Sadaqah Jariya projects am I involved in?	

Month	
Are there any family members, relatives, friends or neighbours going through financial difficulty?	Yes / No
Am I supporting my local Mosque?	Yes / No
Which Dawah projects am I supporting?	
Where in the world am I helping those in need?	
What Sadaqah Jariya projects am I involved in?	

The Divine Decree: Finding peace through acceptance

Month	
Are there any family members, relatives, friends or neighbours going through financial difficulty?	Yes / No
Am I supporting my local Mosque?	Yes / No
Which Dawah projects am I supporting?	
Where in the world am I helping those in need?	
What Sadaqah Jariya projects am I involved in?	

Month	
Are there any family members, relatives, friends or neighbours going through financial difficulty?	Yes / No
Am I supporting my local Mosque?	Yes / No
Which Dawah projects am I supporting?	
Where in the world am I helping those in need?	
What Sadaqah Jariya projects am I involved in?	

What non-financial acts of charity have I done today?	Date

The Divine Decree: Finding peace through acceptance

What non-financial acts of charity have I done today?	Date

What non-financial acts of charity have I done today?	Date

The Divine Decree: Finding peace through acceptance

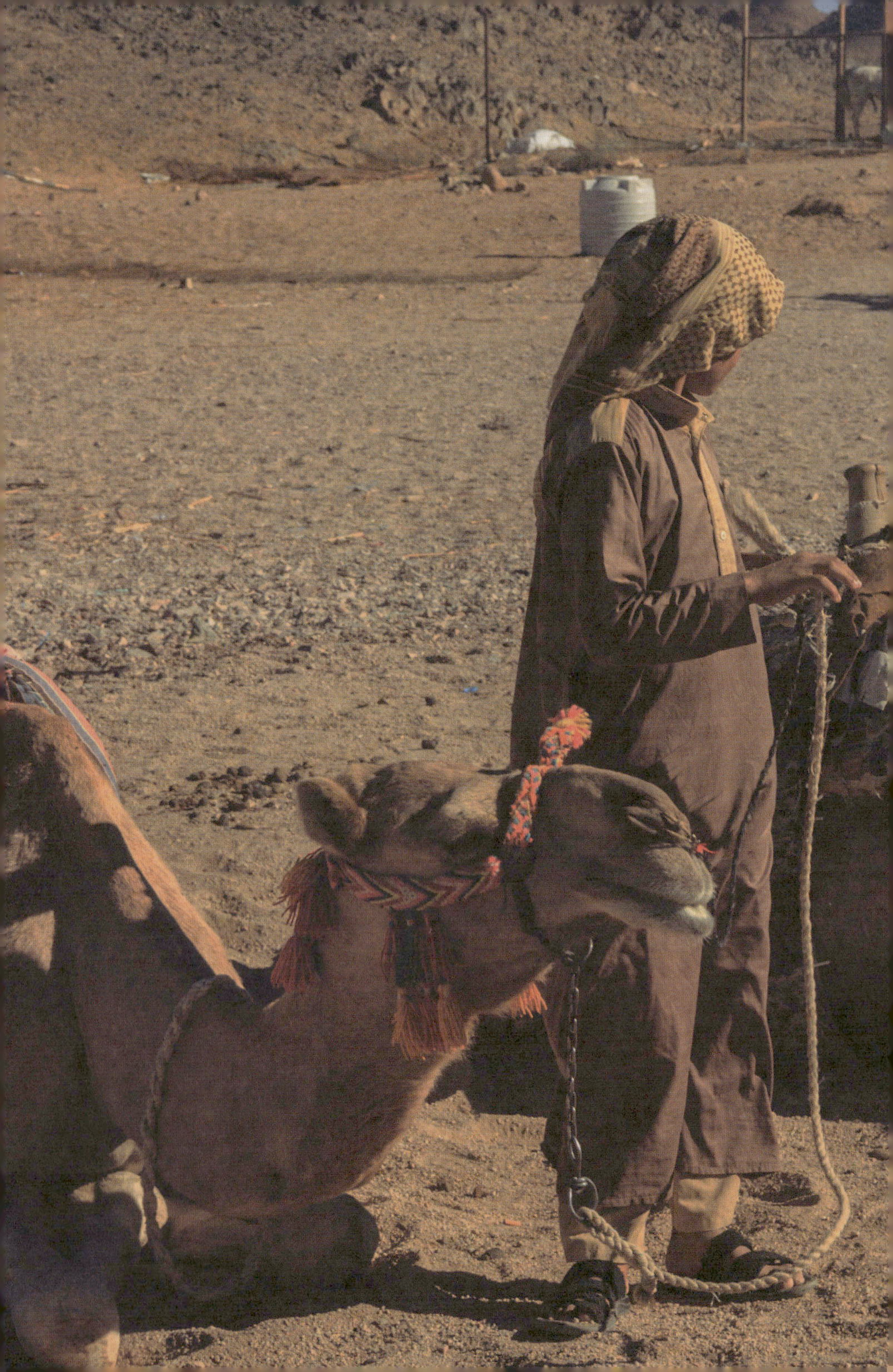

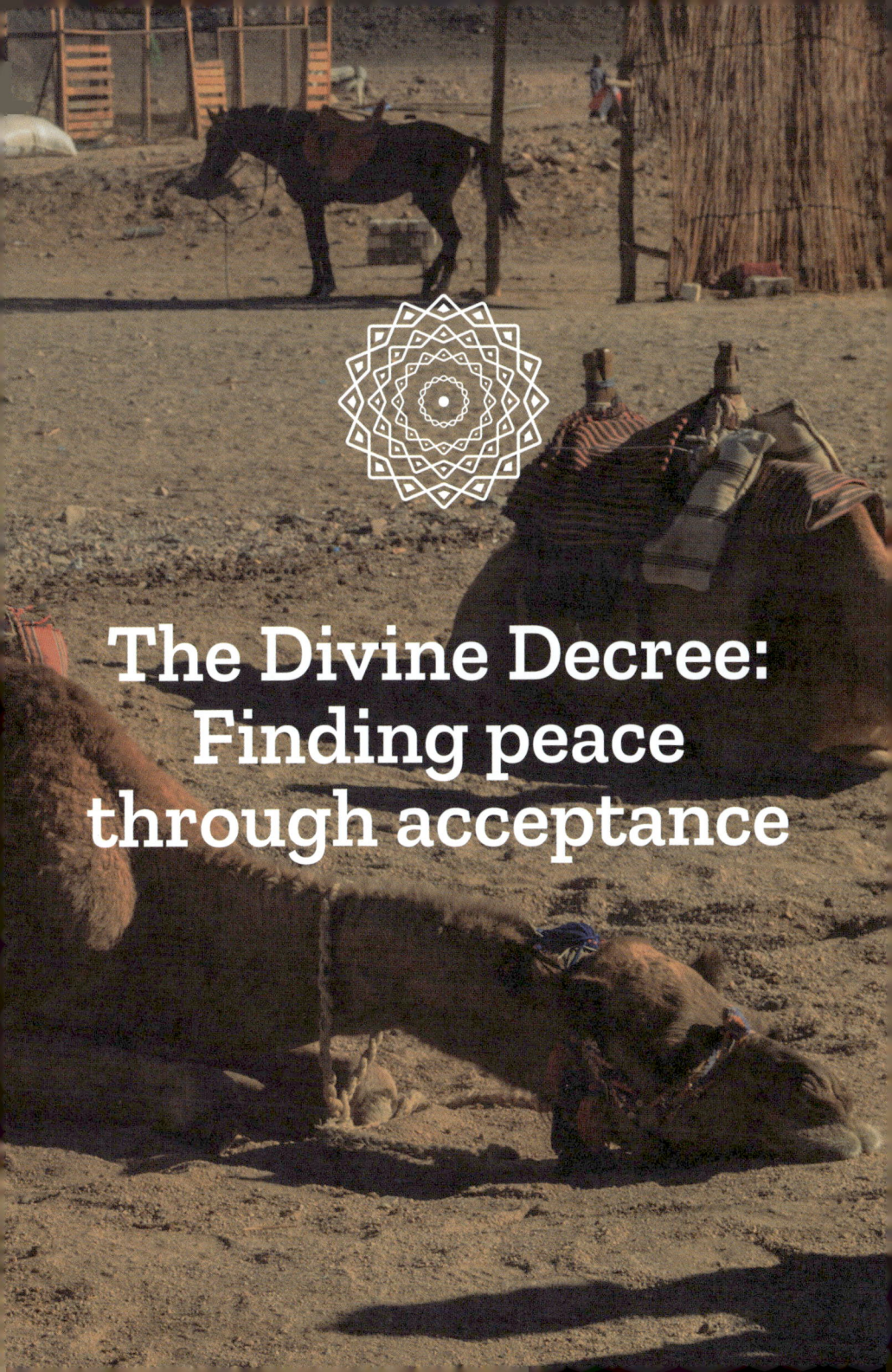

The Divine Decree: Finding peace through acceptance

Everyone has their own stresses and difficulties

We often look at others, sometimes people we know (friends or relatives) or people we know about (celebrities, sports stars, business people) and fantasise about how stress-free and enjoyable their life must be. We assume they do not face the same kind of difficulties and stresses that affect us. We like to imagine how happy we would be if we were in their shoes.

What we fail to realise is that everyone has their own problems no matter how happy they appear, how strong their relationships seem, how wealthy they are, or what kind of job they have. If we were to spend some time talking to them, finding out what is going on in their lives, we would realise that no-one is without worries and troubles. Often-times we will end up feeling glad we are not that person or in their situation, our troubles will seem less difficult in comparison.

This life is a test

What we must remember is that our life in this world is a test from Allah, and our purpose is not to live a life of ease and pleasure but to pass this test. The better we are doing, the stronger our faith the more difficult this test becomes. As Allah says in the Qur'an:

> *You will certainly be tested through your wealth and persons... (Qur'an 3:186)*

> *We will certainly test you: with fear, hunger, loss of wealth, health and harvests. Give good news to the patient... (Qur'an 2:155)*

> *The Prophet (peace be upon him) was asked, "O Messenger of Allah, which people are tested most severely?" The Prophet (peace be upon him) said, "They are the Prophets, then the next best, then the next best. A man is tried according to his religion. If he is firm in his religion, then his trials will be more severe." (Tirmidhi)*

Therefore, we have to change the way we think. We cannot expect to live a life free of troubles, Allah has reserved that for Paradise, for those who pass the trials and tribulations of this life.

Once we do this we will stop expecting our life to be constantly full of joy and happiness and start to expect there to be times of hardship. In this way, when we next enter a period of our life when we face trouble, when something goes wrong, we will not overreact and complain. We will not become depressed and start questioning Allah – 'Why me?' because we will understand that this is a normal part of life. We will realise times of hardship and trouble will occur, and we will have to deal with them in the same way every other person has to.

The will of Allah

Following this, we need to change the way we think about the hardships we face. We must remember that everything that happens is by the will of Allah. Let us imagine some examples of extremely difficult and distressing situations, e.g. getting divorced, going bankrupt, becoming homeless, or losing a close family member, such as a sibling, parent or child.

When devastating things like this happen we often blame ourselves or others. What we must realise is that when something has happened, it has been revealed to us that this was the will of Allah. It is revealed to us that it was decided by Allah and written in 'al-Lauh al-Mahfuz' (The Preserved Tablet / The Book of Decrees) even before He created the Universe. Therefore, whatever happens was always going to happen, there was no way it could have been avoided. As Allah says in the Qur'an:

> *Any disaster on Earth or to yourselves is written down before it happens; this is easy for Allah.* (Qur'an 57:22)

This means we must not think that we could have avoided a difficulty had we done something differently. The Prophet (peace be upon him) warned us against this:

> *"If a calamity befalls you, do not say, 'If only I had done that, it would have been like that.' Say instead, 'It is the destiny of Allah and He does whatever He wishes' for surely 'if' opens the door for Shaitan."* (Muslim)

Is there benefit in the harm?

Alongside changing our mindset to expecting hardships and troubles to come our way from time to time, and accepting the reality of predestination, we must also consider what purpose these trials and tribulations serve. The Prophet (peace be upon him) told us:

> *"How wonderful is the affair of the believer, for his affairs are all good, and this applies to no one but the believer. If something good happens to him, he is thankful for it and that is good for him. If something bad happens to him, he bears it with patience and that is good for him."* (Muslim)

This leads us to another fundamental concept of our faith; Allah loves each and every one of us. To understand how much, consider the following story:

"Some prisoners were brought to the Prophet (peace be upon him), and there was a woman among them who was searching for her child. When she found him, she embraced him and put him to her breast. The Prophet (peace be upon him) said to his disciples (may Allah be pleased with them all), 'Do you think that this woman would throw her child in the fire?' They said, 'No, by Allah, not if she is able not to.' The Prophet (peace be upon him) said, 'Allah is more merciful to His slaves than this woman is to her child.'" (Bukhari)

If we truly believe and understand this, then how can anything that befalls us by the will of Allah be harmful for us?

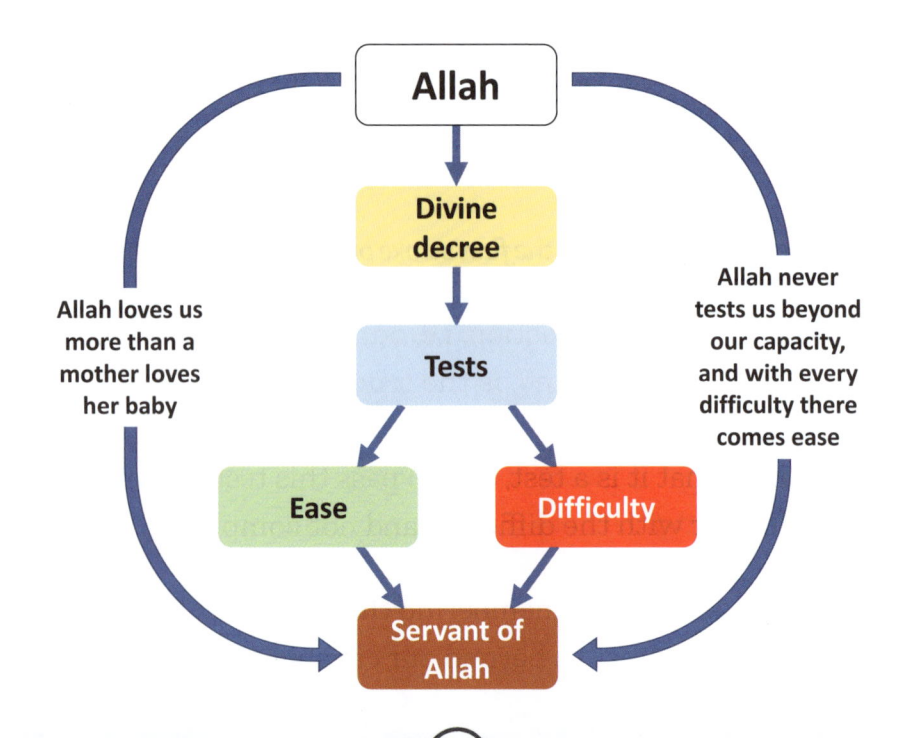

Allah

↓

Divine decree

↓

Tests

↙ ↘

Ease   **Difficulty**

↘ ↙

Servant of Allah

Allah loves us more than a mother loves her baby

Allah never tests us beyond our capacity, and with every difficulty there comes ease

Sabr, Shukr and Istighfar

When we face a difficulty in our life, to understand how it is beneficial for us we must consider three things; Sabr (patience), Shukr (gratitude), and Istighfar (repentance).

❖ **Sabr – having patience and remaining steadfast**

With regards to patience, Allah mentions this quality 90 times in the Quran. In one verse He specifically singles it out to give it the highest honour:

Believers, find strength through patience and prayer - Allah is with those who are patient. (Qur'an 2:153)

But as the Prophet (peace be upon him) told us:

"The real patience is at the first stroke of a calamity." (Bukhari)

This means our initial reaction, i.e. our first thoughts and what we say and do at that time, is the true test of whether we are patient or not. Therefore, whenever we are in difficulty we have to remember that it is a test, and to pass this test we have to be patient, to bear with the difficulty and not complain.

This is made easier by remembering that Allah, our Creator and Sustainer, will not test us beyond our capability:

Allah does not burden anyone beyond their capacity... (Qur'an 2:286)

...Our Lord, do not burden us with more than we can bear, pardon us, forgive us and be kind to us. (Qur'an 2:286)

❖ Shukr – gratitude to Allah

Now let us consider something even higher than bearing a difficulty with patience, and that is to express gratitude to Allah. To be able to do this we have to realise that everything that happens to us, not just the things we like, but both the good and what we think of as bad, is in fact good for us and a blessing from Allah.

This is a difficult concept to understand so let us go back to the examples of life's calamities I mentioned earlier. Consider losing a child, how could this be a blessing from Allah? One way is that when we have patience, when we realise this is Allah's will and accept it, that it was Allah who gave us our child and our child was Allah's to take away, then Allah is pleased with us, our sins are forgiven, and our rank is raised. As Allah says in the Qur'an:

...Give good news to the patient and who, when they are struck by misfortune, softly say: "We belong to Allah and are returning to Him". These are the ones who shall be blessed and will be taken care of by their Lord; they are the guided. (Qur'an 2:155-157)

The Prophet (peace be upon him) told us:

> *"When a person's child dies, Allah the Most High, asks His Angels, 'Have you taken the life of My slave's child?' They reply that they have. He then asks, 'Have you taken the fruit of his heart?' They reply that they have. Then He asks, 'What has My slave said?' They say: 'He has praised You and said: Inna lillahi wa inna ilaihi raji'un (we belong to Allah and to Him we will return)'. Allah says: 'Build a house for My slave in Jannah (Paradise) and name it Bait'al-Hamd (the House of Praise).'"* (Tirmidhi)

Furthermore:

> *"There is no Muslim that is afflicted with a calamity, and he says what Allah has commanded him to say: "To Allah we belong and to him we will return! O Allah! Give me the rewards (of being patient over) this calamity, and grant me something better than it to replace it," except that Allah will give him something better to replace it."* (Muslim)

So this is one way a calamity can be a blessing; through our patience and reliance on Allah our rank is raised and He is pleased with us. In fact, through our patience He will replace what we have lost with something even better.

Another way is that Allah may have averted a larger calamity that was going to befall us by testing us with a smaller calamity.

What if our child had grown up and left Islam and died as a non-Muslim (Kafir)? They would have entered Hell for all eternity. By dying during childhood they are guaranteed Paradise, where we will have the chance to meet with them again. We can see examples of this in the Qur'an in the stories of Syedina Khidr and the Prophet Moses (peace be upon them both).

The problem is that we are short sighted and do not rely on Allah's infinite wisdom. We do not truly believe that the difficulties we face are beneficial for us because we do not consider what kind of bigger trials and tribulations He may have exposed us to. As He says in the Qur'an:

> *...Sometimes, you may dislike something that is good for you, and sometimes you may like something that is bad for you. Only Allah knows the whole truth, not you. (Quran 2:216)*

One of the Awliyah-Allah used to make a Dua in which he said:

> *"I make Dua to Allah for something I want, and if He gives it to me then I am happy once, and if He does not give it to me then I am happy ten times because the first was my choice, but the second was Allah's choice."*

As the Prophet (peace be upon him) told us:

> *"Whatever Allah has decreed for His believing slave is a blessing, even if that is in the form of withholding; it*

is a favour even if that is in the form of a trial; and the calamity decreed by Him is fair, even if it is painful." (Madarij al-Salikeen)

Indeed, by being grateful we call the blessings of Allah down upon ourselves, as He said in the Quran:

...If you are grateful, I will surely increase My favours to you, but if you are ungrateful, then My punishment is severe. (Qur'an 14:7)

❖ Istighfar – seeking forgiveness for our many sins

Having discussed patience and gratitude, the third aspect is Istighfar (to seek forgiveness/repentance). This involves two things, the first is to realise that our sins can result in punishment in this life as well as in the grave and the Hereafter. This does not mean that every difficulty we face is a punishment but a Muslim understands that it is only the Prophets who are free from sin. However pious others may believe us to be, the closer we get to Allah the more we realise how sinful we are. Therefore, when faced with a difficulty a Muslim should consider that it could be a punishment and seek forgiveness from Allah.

This is exemplified in the story of Taif, the most difficult time in the Prophet's life, when he was rudely rejected by the chieftains and physically assaulted by being pelted with stones until his shoes filled with blood. In his supplication to Allah, he said, "So long as You are not angry with me, I do not care." Therefore, even in the case of the Prophet, his only concern after such a terrible ordeal is that the calamity befell him as a result of Allah's displeasure, which of course was not the case.

However, even if the difficulty is not a punishment, by exhibiting the qualities of patience and gratitude, some of our sins are forgiven. As the Prophet (peace be upon him) told us:

> *"No fatigue, nor disease, nor sorrow, nor sadness, nor hurt, nor distress befalls a Muslim, even if it were the prick he receives from a thorn, but that Allah expiates some of his sins for that." (Bukhari)*

> *"Trials will continue to befall the believing man and woman, with regard to themselves, their children and their wealth, until they meet Allah with no sin on them." (Tirmidhi)*

The second benefit of repentance in times of difficulty is explained by the following Hadith:

> *"Whoever increases his prayers for forgiveness, Allah will grant him relief from every worry, a way out from every hardship, and provide for him in ways he does not expect." (Ahmad)*

So when we seek repentance in times of difficulty (not that this should be the only time we do Istighfar – the Prophet would do so at least 100 times each day), it should be with the sincere belief that Allah will help us through the difficulty, the test that He is putting us through. As He says in the Qur'an:

> *Indeed, every hardship is followed by ease, indeed, every hardship is followed by ease. (Qur'an 94:5-6)*

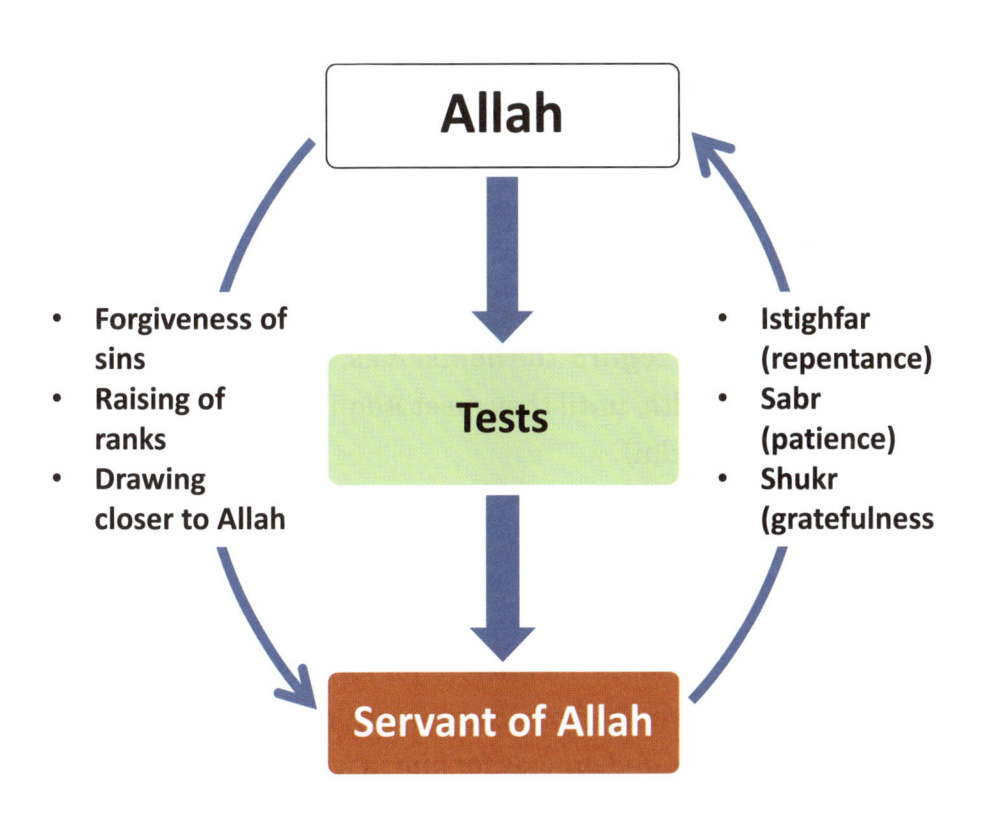

```
                    ┌─────────────┐
                    │    Allah    │
                    └─────────────┘
                           │
                           ▼
                    ┌─────────────┐
                    │    Tests    │
                    └─────────────┘
                           │
                           ▼
                    ┌─────────────────┐
                    │ Servant of Allah│
                    └─────────────────┘
```

- **Forgiveness of sins**
- **Raising of ranks**
- **Drawing closer to Allah**

- **Istighfar (repentance)**
- **Sabr (patience)**
- **Shukr (gratefulness)**

Summary

I have talked about changing our mindset so we expect hardships and troubles to come our way from time to time; and also to realise that the hardships we face are the will of Allah and predestined for us. I have discussed how Allah's love for us is greater than even that of a mother for her child and that everything that happens to a believer is a blessing for him. This is by having patience and considering that Allah may have spared us from an even greater test, which we may not have been able to bear and may have even put our faith in jeopardy. It is also by realising that through these tests we can achieve higher ranks and get closer to Allah. Through this patience, Allah will replace what we have lost with something even better. Therefore, not only do we exhibit patience but we also express gratitude; in His infinite wisdom Allah knows what is best for us. When we express gratitude we gain even greater pleasure of Allah and He showers even more of His blessings upon us. Through these difficulties Allah also cleanses us of our sins so we can stand before him on the Day of Judgement in a purified state and, by His grace, enter His Paradise where we will spend eternity in peace and comfort.

The purpose of this chapter is to provide a practical means of reflecting upon and appreciating the immeasurable blessings of Allah upon us even in times of difficulty and stress. We can fill in the blank tables on the following pages with lists of things we are grateful for, what difficulties we are currently facing and whether these outweigh all that Allah has given us. Furthermore, we should reflect upon the difficulties we face and consider what benefits and blessings are hidden within these tests Allah has bestowed upon us. Doing this exercise regularly, especially in times of difficulty and stress, will help develop a habit of patience and gratitude.

What am I grateful for? What do I thank Allah for?

The Divine Decree: Finding peace through acceptance

What am I grateful for? What do I thank Allah for?

What am I grateful for? What do I thank Allah for?

The Divine Decree: Finding peace through acceptance

What difficulties am I facing?	Do these outweigh the blessings Allah has bestowed upon me?
	Yes / No
	Yes / No
	Yes / No
	Yes / No
	Yes / No
	Yes / No
	Yes / No
	Yes / No
	Yes / No
	Yes / No

What difficulties am I facing?	Do these outweigh the blessings Allah has bestowed upon me?
	Yes / No
	Yes / No
	Yes / No
	Yes / No
	Yes / No
	Yes / No
	Yes / No
	Yes / No
	Yes / No
	Yes / No

The Divine Decree: Finding peace through acceptance

What difficulties am I facing?	Do these outweigh the blessings Allah has bestowed upon me?
	Yes / No
	Yes / No
	Yes / No
	Yes / No
	Yes / No
	Yes / No
	Yes / No
	Yes / No
	Yes / No
	Yes / No

What blessings of Allah are hidden in the difficulties I am facing?

The Divine Decree: Finding peace through acceptance

What blessings of Allah are hidden in the difficulties I am facing?

What blessings of Allah are hidden in the difficulties I am facing?

The Divine Decree: Finding peace through acceptance